MW00649921

Dr. Robert
Pierson

tell

How to
Share Your Faith
With Others

What Others Say About "Tell"

In my view there are only two or three truly great books on personal witnessing that have come out recent enough to consider the complex age that we live today. Tell, by Dr. Robert Pierson is one of those books. It brings clarity to complexity and adds a touch of practicality to sharing the Good News that is missing in so many recently written theoretical books. But best of all, Tell motivates the reader to reach out into the community and become missional. It put a fire in my soul and I expect to see that fire catch on in my church and my community.

Dr. Tim White, Senior Pastor
Washington Cathedral, Redmond WA
Adjunct Professor at Northwest University, Kirkland WA

"Bob's, and my, denomination is devoting great energy and expense in attempting to reverse current statistical trends. However, we don't find much mention of evangelism in all this, when it should be foundational to any renewal strategy. Bob's book is a timely and valuable resource which will hopefully call us back to informed and equipped action in the "last will and testament" of Jesus."

Rev. Dr. John H. Southwick,
Director of Research
General Board of Global Ministries of the United Methodist Church

"Bob Pierson's new book on the ministry of evangelism is one of the most readable and engaging in years. More important, it builds on vast experience in churches and communities, and with lost people who needed to be found. Most important, the book is often so specific that you will actually know what to do; and if, on occasion, you disagree—you will think of a better way, at least for you!"

George Hunter III,
Professor of Evangelism and Church Growth
Asbury Theological Seminary, United Methodist Church

What Others Say About "Tell"

I am happy and privileged to endorse the new book by Bob Pierson called, Tell. *The author of Needs Based Evangelism had added this book to illuminate his obvious passion of evangelism.*

The book is all about the use of story-telling in different ways for different circumstances. Bob artfully weaves biblical stories with true life stories of today. He carefully points the reader to the fact that our day is a very different day from that of Bible times, however the power of story-telling is just as effective. The book becomes a pragmatic how-to for Christians in the art of witnessing. Following Bob's examples helps to bring back the enthusiasm and simplicity exemplified by those early believers in Bible times. The secret of that excitement was in seeing others grasp the truths of the Gospel applied to their lives. Bob, "makes the message plain" and leads by example. He draws out the overriding truth of God's love and grace. His 50 years of pastoral ministry is distilled in this work. It is all about Jesus.

Rev. Dr. Lawrence Wilkes,
President, California Graduate School of Theology
President, Okanagan Bible College/
Canadian Graduate School of Ministry

"The journey toward faithful discipleship must include the winsome invitation for others to also join the journey. Bob Pierson gives an artful blend of both inspiration and instruction for every church that seeks to fruitfully respond to Jesus' Great Commission. This is a must-read book for the 21st century Christian."

Bob Crossman,
Conference UMC Minister of New Church Starts and
Congregational Advancement
Arkansas Conference UMC

What Others Say About "Tell"

"If your church needs a resource to inspire, motive and train people to bring others to Christ, this is it. Bob is a captivating, narrative writer whose passion for introducing others to Christ is contagious. His lifetime of learning offers tremendous insight."

Jessica Moffatt-Seay,
Senior Pastor
First UMC Ardmore, Oklahoma

We have a story to tell and a Christ to share. Bob Pierson's book, Tell, gives the disciple of Christ the proper tools and challenge to offer Christ to all that we meet. My dear friend Bob makes it clear that the Great Commission is not an option but it is what the Lord expects all who confess Him to be Lord and Savior to do. I recommend this book to all who are serious about making disciples for Jesus Christ and use its practical applications in sharing the Gospel with others! With the world in the state in which it is, we cannot waste anymore time! It's time for us to Tell the story!

Tyrone D. Gordon,
Senior Pastor, St. Luke "Community" United Methodist Church
Dallas, Texas

Every time I talk to Bob Pierson, his heart for people to know Jesus is overwhelmingly evident. How God has used him in churches he has been in leadership of has shown this is his passion. This book gives practical insight to his passion and for seeing lives changed as people understand the saving grace of Jesus and put faith in Him.

Dan Kimball,
Vintage Faith Church
Author of *They Like Jesus But Not the Church* and
The Emerging Church: Vintage Christianity for New Generations

Contents

Acknowledgments

In putting together this whole TELL effort, I particularly appreciate the many church leaders, clergy, and laity who have given me advice, counsel, and encouragement as I worked on this project. I also appreciate all of those colleagues who have been a part of our common task to find effective ways for Christians to share their faith in a sometimes very secular world. In the preparation of the manuscript, I particularly appreciate those who have directly done editorial work, manuscript preparation—Jessica Decker and Jamie Pierson for their work and suggestions. I appreciate the help of Bob Crossman. I so deeply appreciate all those who have provided endorsements for this book. Their words make this effort so valuable. Particularly, I appreciate Kent Mallard, whose first suggestion and invitation started me on this journey to prepare the book, *Tell*. The task of this book was done only with much prayer, thought, and a conviction that this is one of the most important tasks that a Christian has to deal with today. I appreciate all those who helped in this journey.

Bob Pierson

Introduction
"Well Done, Good and Faithful Servant"

This book is written out of the conviction that God calls us to do His will, follow His teachings, help, love, care, learn, and do.

We Are Called

I was in my third semester at Oklahoma University studying to be an industrial management engineer. I had a room in Whitehurst Hall, one of the older dormitories at OU. It was dingy and not very comfortable, but I was excited to be studying to join the ranks of successful engineers. I loved engineering, science and math, and it seemed right that I should be an engineer. That night I was reading the popular magazine *LIFE*. The article was about nuclear weapons, war and the current development of technology. As much as I loved technology, as I read the story in *LIFE* magazine my life was changed. As I read the story about the development of nuclear technology and what that would mean for the future of humanity, I realized how critically important it was for us to develop our technology in helping, loving, caring and how important the positive truth of Christ was in the midst of the threats of war and a possible nuclear holocaust.

The decision I made that night was to change vocations and my direction in life. Not that there was anything wrong with being an engineer, but I felt clearly that I needed to be a minister of the Gospel of Jesus Christ. I was being called to help people. To lead people to have values, find truth, to love, to help each other and to help others find God. Simply I was called to help make the world better. I heard God call to me and I knew that my job was making disciples of Christ. That was what I was supposed to do full time as my vocation. When I made that decision I found a deep sense of peace, joy and a desire to do my best. I knew God was directing the decision. I was at peace and empowered.

This is the simple story of my decision to become a pastor. It is a story of an individual who felt God's call and made a total commitment. Most Christians have stories of the decision they made to become a Christian. Others have stories of decisions they made to become a better Christian or to correct a serious problem in their life. Many could tell their story about overcoming addictions, becoming a better parent, working to bring social justice, help the poor or committing a significant portion of their time to the church.

Jesus described His call in Luke 4:18–19 as *"The Spirit of the Lord is on me, because he has anointed me to preach good news to the poor. He has sent me to proclaim freedom for the prisoners and recovery of sight for the blind, to release the oppressed, to proclaim the year of the Lord's favor."*

The beautiful thing about the way God works with us is that we are given free will with the call. God encourages us in every way imaginable, but the free will to make the choice is ours. The second beautiful thing about the story is that the decision to follow Jesus Christ at any level at any time is joyful, empowering, encouraging and leads to a deep sense of inner peace. It is the power of God's Spirit. It is really a good deal!

This book is about that good life and how to share it. It is about God's call. This book is a practical guide to sharing the faith in Jesus Christ.

Our Response

There's a biblical phrase in the twenty-fifth chapter of Matthew; it is precious to any person who has accepted Jesus Christ as their Lord and Savior. Jesus is telling the story of the talents. In the story, when one of the particular individuals returns, the master says, *"Well done, good and faithful servant"* (Matthew 25:21,23). To have

Christ speak to us and say, "Well done, good and faithful servant" is the best thing anyone could ask for. Certainly, God is a God of grace and forgiveness who forgives our mistakes and our bungling, our poor results and our half-baked ideas. This book is about our response.

Jesus said to the disciples He called by Lake Galilee at the beginning of His ministry, *"Come, follow me, and I will make you fishers of men"* (Matt. 4:19). This book is about doing that very thing: leading people to Christ. In our desire to be a good disciple or good leader, we want to do what He told us to do. The words at the end of Matthew 28:19–20 are called the Great Commission. Jesus makes it clear: *"Therefore go and make disciples of all nations, baptizing them in the name of the Father and of the Son and of the Holy Spirit, and teaching them to obey everything I have commanded you. And surely I am with you always, to the very end of the age."* This book is about doing what He said and trusting that His affirmation will be upon us, "Well done, good and faithful servant."

In the biblical story of Andrew found in John 1:40–50, we have the simple excitement of Andrew telling his brother Simon about Jesus, and then later the same experience as Phillip tells Nathanael about Him as well. In each case, you can sense the excitement of Andrew and Phillip as they tell. We are called to do the same thing. We are called to tell about Jesus!

The TELLers

Eddy and Patty are bikers. Eddy's vocation is a barber; Patty suffers from multiple sclerosis. She rides with him on the bike, and they love Jesus. Patty, in dealing with her disease, and Eddy, in wrestling with his calling, both believe that they're called to share Jesus Christ with others. They have found such power, help and meaning in following Christ that they want to share. They want to share with their biker friends. They want to share with people they know and meet. They are so excited about being Christians and following Christ that they must find a way to tell others.

Doug is a doctor who went through a tough divorce; before and after this, he was a committed agnostic. So, in his singleness, he wandered and struggled. His son invited him to a Christian concert. At the concert, God began to touch Doug's life. In the months that followed, Doug eventually came to believe in the message of Jesus; but his commitment was not only to believe but to be a person who wanted to share this good news. Doug understood that, the good news in his personal life changed him so much. He followed the rules of Jesus to rebuild his life. He now sees himself as a leader in his church, and as a professional in the community. He's seeking to find a way in this crazy culture to be an evangelist.

Becky is a young adult who is a pastor of a church. She cares about the people of her generation and is involved in conversation with other young Christians who describe themselves as a part of the emergent church movement. She seeks to find a way to bring new people to Jesus. She struggles to find the effective ways to reach her generation.

Larry is a leader of a denomination; he served as a pastor for many years and now, as a significant leader of a denomination that is declining rapidly. He seeks to find the answers. Why, what has changed, how do we bring the message of Jesus to a rapidly changing culture? As a leader he is asking, "How do we help the mainline church?"

These five people of four different generations are all seeking to find the ways to share this beautiful truth that Jesus brought as a gift from God to the rest of humanity. They're not mean or arrogant or close-minded or even hypocritical; they are genuine Christian human beings who are trying to do what Jesus Christ taught. They are honest people whose lives have been radically influenced by the message of love that Jesus brought to Galilee so long ago. They are excited about sharing this good news. This book is about their struggle, and every other American Christian's struggle, on how to share the faith.

Understand the Changing Culture

This book is about sharing the faith in a changing culture. "Things are changing." That's a simple phrase that we oftentimes hear. We recognize that our culture has shifted. It's not only because of the advancements in technology that has brought a whole new way of doing so many things, from communications to transportation. It is a change within our culture that has changed our lifestyle, our families, our ways of relating to others. A change in our culture that has transformed the way we relate to the world, the way we understand values, the way we express our beliefs.

To put it simply, we are now, in the United States, in a post-Christian era. Other places in the western world have gone through that same kind of change, sometime in the last 20 years. This could be described in terms of postmodern philosophy, or simply a secular emphasis that has come to dominate our culture. The culture is different. However sociologists or anthropologists want to describe the change in our culture, Christian leaders, ministers and rank-and-file have found themselves in a different world. Like tourists who visited another continent and another culture, we find ourselves as Christians in a very secular world that is in many ways radically different from what we understand Jesus Christ taught. What a truly Christian culture would look like is a subject for much debate. Without debating all the aspects, both theological, behavioral, moral and social, we realize that things are significantly different.

Christians wrestle with the divine imperative that Jesus gave the last time that He spoke to the disciples. He gathered his leaders and presented what has been called the Great Commission. He told them to go make disciples. Emil Brunner coined the term "Divine Imperative" to describe this instruction in his book of the same title, and it has stuck. We have done it. Missionaries have been sent around the world. Evangelists have preached from street corners and hometown football stadiums, and people have come to follow the teachings of Jesus Christ. They have accepted Christ as their Lord and Savior. Christians have acted with the passion and care that Christ exhibited and called us to have. The vision of a world of peace and the call to responsibility and integrity has been the Christian standard. This worldview is deeply a part of what Christians believe Jesus taught. Christians believe they are greatly needed in the midst of our contemporary situation.

There have been in the past and there are presently secular worldviews that place the priority upon our own self-centeredness, our own arrogance. There is meanness. Persons want to get everything for themselves rather than helping others. Truth becomes only a pragmatic idea; only our opinion for the moment as we want something for ourselves. We so often lack values, integrity, responsibility, love and human justice.

Those of us who know that they must follow the imperative that Jesus gave on the mountain as He said goodbye to His disciples find ourselves without tools and understanding of how to share and are bewildered and frustrated. We find ourselves called hypocrites and closed-minded. This book is dedicated to helping Christians who truly are following Jesus Christ and His way of love to share His message and His truth. The goal is to share with our friends, family and anyone we meet in a way that is not obnoxious, mean or derogatory, but is helpful and loving and joyful.

My friend was called to be a missionary. He trained to go to Africa to share the faith. A part of his training and the training of every missionary was to understand the culture, language, history, expectations, family systems and even the government of the countries that he was to share Christ in. He had to learn how to share Christ in a way that the people of that culture would understand. Today, the Christians in the United States find themselves as missionaries in sometimes very un-Christian places. In the midst of this, we need to be as intentional, energetic, determined and caring as any of the great missionaries who brought the Gospel at the time of the great missionary movement around the world. The enthusiasm of the Chinese Christians worshipping in a house church needs to be ours. The dedication and commitment of new Christians in parts of Africa today should be ours. The enthusiasm of those who found the power of Christ all across South America needs to become the new motivation for Christians in the United States, who are finding that they are living in a world that so aggressively would seek to contradict the ethics, love, justice, hope and truth of Jesus Christ.

Instructions

This book is dedicated to helping us share the Gospel, to share it in a way that is effective. We are called to share it in a way that is consistent with the teachings of Jesus Christ, not only in terms of particular theological understanding of the nature of God but in terms of psychological understandings of how we treat our neighbors. The Great Commandments call us to love God and love our neighbors as ourselves; that's the theological basis for the chapters of this book. The Great Commandments and the Great Commission are the essential theological undergirding of what is shared here. This method of evangelism is based upon Christ's method of evangelism. In order to understand how to share it, we must begin by understanding how powerful the message of Jesus Christ is today.

The first part of the book describes an outline for individuals to be prepared. Chapters 6 through 10 give instructions for the individual to tell others about committing their lives to Christ. The other chapters provide theological and practical context for telling about the power of accepting and following Christ.

Chapters 13 through 17 in the second half of the book talk about how a local church empowers the individual to tell others about Christ. These chapters outline the local church program of evangelism. There is associated with the materials a manual for planning a ten-week program called Ten to Tell that helps a church effectively make the emphasis upon evangelism. A journal is provided to help you keep track of those that you're sharing with and witnessing to. There's a manual that instructs us on how to carry out the principles of TELL on an individual basis as we witness to our friends and acquaintances. We are called to be prepared.

The book is written in a way that it can be read from a variety of points of view. It can be simply a study book for your own personal enrichment. It can also be a book to be read with a group, in a Bible study, Sunday school class or accountability group. The questions at the end of each chapter can be useful for both personal reflection and group discussion. The book is also written in a way that it can become a study book for those who want to develop their skills in sharing the faith. Later in the book, I will suggest ways that people can gather together as a group and help each other in learning how to share their faith. Simple exercises and activities that can help develop your evangelistic skills are part of the latter part of the book. It's hoped that you will use those skill development aspects not only as a set of exercise for you and several of your fellow Christians to do together. The individual reader can also enter into those exercises on a very personal basis. The book is written in the hopes that all readers find their own ways in sharing the faith, ways that work. I suggest that you create a kind of prayer journal listing people that you're sharing with, how you're sharing, what you're saying. Journal what works as well as what does not work. As you read through the book, I hope that it can therefore become usable in all kinds of ways in the life of the Church.

As you read the book, it will only be meaningful if you read and pray. Would you pray and ask for understanding and guidance? The book is written in a way that I hope can be used by your local church, your class, your Bible study group, your friends. It is not necessarily a lockstep manual, but it's a set of ideas to help us to tell the truth. That truth has changed my life and is the driving force in my writing and my sharing. I pray that it is yours.

Dr. Robert Pierson

Chapter 1

How Good It Is!

It was one of those unusual moments that happen, particularly in a pastor's life. I was making a hospital call to a loyal church member. Bob was a charter member of my church, taught the largest, most vital Sunday School class in the church, had been chairman of several of the committees, including the Social Action Committee, and he was dying of cancer. I remember he was in a great deal of pain, and, yet, when I came into the room, Bob wanted to talk. His words were strained, but clear. He said simply, "Tell 'em how good it is." I said, "What do you mean?" He replied, with an energy that overcame his pain, "I mean, tell them how good it is to follow Jesus." I replied back, "Of course!" He then grabbed a hold of my hand and held it with a grip that almost cut off circulation. He said, "Tell them at my funeral how great it is to be a Christian and to serve God and follow Jesus. Will you tell them?" There was so much I wanted to say to him at that point. I knew how great the pain was, and I simply said, "Yes, yes. I will tell them." Bob, on his death bed, made it clear what all of us who have committed our lives to Christ know. It is a fantastic experience!

Not long after I committed my life as a minister I ran out of money to go to college. My uncle Lee invited me to come to west Texas. He would find me a job where I could earn enough money to go back to school. Lee was a great salesman. He told me he could get me a job working for his insurance company and he did. He convinced both me and the insurance company that I could sell. He taught me how. Among the things he taught was to be clear about the benefits of the product, how good it is, how it helps and how it will make a difference. We need to be clear about the fantastic benefits of following Jesus.

tell

Lee said if you want to sell insurance you need to explain the benefits. If you want to tell what it means to be a Christian, the best resource we have is our own story of all the benefits. At the time of writing this book I have been a pastor for over 50 years.

We must make it clear how good it is! Often our story of God's call is filled with the experience of sacrifice and dedication, of work and hardship, of how hard it is to follow His call, and we fail to tell how great it is. We seldom celebrate how much fun it is to be a Christian. The emphasis on the seriousness sometimes takes away the emphasis on the joy. It is wonderful to follow Jesus!

As a young pastor in Tulsa, Oklahoma, I became friends with a very successful oil man. He had made lots of money; he was tough, rugged and successful. But in mid-life, Bill decided to sell out his interest in the oil company and take all his money and spend the rest of his life giving it away. What could change a man so radically that he would change from a successful entrepreneur to a magnificent benefactor for countless organizations and individuals? Bill Broadhurst gave money to colleges and universities all over the country. He supported Christian institutions of all kinds, including being the founder of the church I came to serve most of my life. He provided money for seminary and college education for countless individuals. Bill loved to give, to help, and he loved Jesus Christ. How could a man change so radically? How could a man give up all the power, influence and success he had in oil production in order to become an individual who helped and gave away millions of dollars? Something really good happened to him. If he were alive to tell you today, he would explain clearly that it was Jesus Christ.

The stories of dramatic examples of what happens to an individual as they follow Christ are legendary, like the story of Albert Switzer, an accomplished musician and famous scientist who became a missionary in Africa, or Mother Teresa giving away her life to help the poor in India. These are just two famous stories of what happens to an individual who comes to follow Jesus Christ. Jesus teaches us that following Him will mean some very simple things: we will love God first. We will love our neighbors as ourselves. That's the kind of people we'll be. We will be people who, as He describes in Matthew 25 and the Great Commandments in Luke 10, that want to do everything we can to help people in need. This is "a wonderful life!"

This book is about witnessing, sharing the faith. Some might even say it is about selling Jesus. In John's gospel Jesus clearly talks about how wonderful, powerful, purposeful and satisfying it is to follow Him. He describes a beautiful scene: *"I am the gate; whoever enters through me will be saved. He will come in and go out, and find pasture."* He concludes with the promise that we *"may have life, and have it to the full"* (John 10:9–10). In chapter 9 He describes his power as *"the light of the world"* (John 9:5). Earlier He described the message as *"I am the light of the world"* (John 8:12). In that same chapter he states "If you continue in my word, you are truly my disciples; and you will know the truth, and the truth will make you free" (John 8:31–32). Let us celebrate how good it is to know Jesus. We need to be able to tell the world how good, powerful, joyful, satisfying and world changing it is to be a follower of Jesus.

Four Gifts of Faith

We might describe how good being a Christian is in terms of four particular, powerful gifts that are given us through the Christian faith. These are four gifts that are essential for personal strength and health; they are aspects of our lives that psychologists have come to understand as essential. They are simply the gift of self-esteem, the gift of purpose, the gift of rules and the gift of power. These are four ways to describe how good it is.

Self-Esteem

One of the greatest needs that all of us have is to know that we are loved–that we are accepted and forgiven. Whether it's the influence of a good friend, the message of a pastor or the help of a therapist, we need to know that we are worthwhile in order to function effectively through the gift of our faith. In the eighth chapter of Romans, Paul gives a beautiful pep talk to any follower of Jesus who begins to be discouraged or depressed. Paul writes in Romans 8:35 (NKJV) and following, *"Who shall separate us from the love of Christ? Shall tribulation or distress or persecution or famine or nakedness or peril or sword?"* Then he writes in the thirty-seventh verse the answer, *"No, in all these things we are more than conquerors through Him who loves us for I am sure that neither death nor life nor angels nor principalities nor things present nor things to come nor height nor depth nor anything else in all of creation will be able to separate us from the love of God in Christ Jesus our Lord."* What a fantastic promise and reminder of how good it is to follow Jesus! Paul puts it bluntly in the twenty-eighth verse of that same chapter when he says, *"We know that in everything God works for good with those who love him, who are called according to his purpose."* Then, in the thirty-first verse, he brings it home clearly, *"What shall we say to this? If God is for us, who can be against us?"* Those Biblical words remind us of how good it really is.

His love for us is the clearest affirmation of our self-esteem. Despite our faults and mistakes, we are loved by the Creator of the universe.

That sense of self-esteem is a message that Jesus Christ has given us so clearly. John 3:16 (NASB) says that, *"God so loved the world, that he gave his only begotten Son."* This text reminds us of God's ultimate love for us. To really understand its power is to understand that God so loves you. It is your name that goes in the place of the world in that Scripture. God's love is for you. Christ died not just for all the world, but he died for you. It is personal; it is God's love for you. You are a person of worth and value. Through Jesus Christ, you can be forgiven. You are a child of God!

David wrote in Psalm 23 (NKJV) a description of how much God loves us. As we read *"the Lord is my Shepherd, I shall not want..."* the promises of God's amazing grace become life giving, hope fulfilling and empowering. We all know that what we need is knowledge that we are loved and that someone will help; and we are not alone. To be a Christian is to know that all the time. Paul described, *"We know that all things work together for good for those who love God, who are called according to his purpose"* (Romans 8:28). Paul wrote in the same chapter that nothing *"will be able to separate us from the love of God in Christ Jesus our Lord"* (Romans 8:39b ESV). These promises tell us of the peace and power that comes from following Christ. Our identity is changed. It is wonderful! What Jesus described He promised as an "abundant life." Those two words seem all too simple to describe all the benefits of being a follower of Christ.

Purpose

Being a Christian gives us a sense of our purpose in life, that we are created for a reason. Jesus says that we are called to take up our cross and follow Him; that we're called to love our neighbors as ourselves. We are called to bring peace on earth. The second gift that is so clearly a part of being a follower of Jesus Christ is to know that our life has purpose and direction.

Viktor Frankl reminds us that people who have a sense of purpose in life are the people who are successful. Frankl was an Austrian psychologist who was taken prisoner by the Nazis during the Second World War. As a prisoner, he observed the worst of all human conditions and noticed that people seemed to be able to survive and overcome in this worst of all conditions if they had a sense of purpose in life. That simple idea was expressed in his book,

Man's Search for Meaning, which he wrote after the war. The book became popular around the war, launched a form of therapy called logotherapy. His emphasis was simple. We are successful Christians with a purpose of following Jesus and living a life of love. Many other therapists, leaders and pastors have used these concepts to help us understand how important purpose in life is.

The gift of purpose is to help us each to know that our life is valuable and we have a direction. Jesus made it clear that we are to take up our cross daily and follow Him. We have a mission to share the Gospel, to make the world better, to help the needy. As we are called when we give our life to Christ so we become people with a destiny, a sense of purpose.

Rules

The third gift, as followers of Jesus Christ, is the teachings of Jesus provide for us a set of rules to live by. Psychologists teach us that one of the greatest difficulties we all have is ambiguity–not knowing what is right and what is wrong. The gift of being a Christian to know what is right, to know what the truth is, to understand that there are certain things that are loving, kind, just and fair, and we're called to live by those principles. The Sermon on the Mount outlines a set of behaviors for a Christian. Paul describes in 1 Corinthians 13 how to love. Romans 12 outlines rules for living. Jesus says in Luke 10 that we are to love our neighbor as ourselves. These rules are put simply, clearly. The gift of being a Christian is to know that there is a truth. We are called to follow that truth.

It is great to be a Christian. As followers of Jesus Christ we have a foundation of morality, a set of rules that give us direction.

One of my doctoral professors and friends was Dr. John Hampton of Oklahoma State University. As an educational psychologist, he had done extensive research on ambiguity, showing over and over that human beings simply have major difficulty with ambiguity. We want to know what to do, what the truth is, what the direction is and, if things are ambiguous, we do everything we can to find the direction, meaning and truth. The Christian is given God's rules—the Great Commandments, *"Love the Lord your God with all your heart, soul, mind, and body, and your neighbor as yourself."* Jesus says, "Do this and you will live." The Sermon on the Mount is filled with direction for life. The teachings of the Bible are filled with direction, truth and morality. As followers of Jesus Christ, we have a foundation of morality, a set of rules that gives us direction.

Power

The fourth gift is power. As individuals, when we get worn out, tired, discouraged or bewildered, we often seek help from friends and family. The Christian knows that we have help not only from friends and family but also from the source of life, the power of universe—God is our power! The Bible teaches us that God's Spirit is with us; it is a part of the gift of following Jesus Christ. Prayer becomes a way in which we access that sense of God's energy and direction in our lives. Jesus says we are not alone. We are encouraged to understand the power of God's Holy Spirit to guide, direct and empower us.

Finally, we need help. We find ourselves running out of resources or experiencing loneliness. In the midst of that, the Christian finds that God is there. God is in the midst of the trouble; God is answering our prayers; God is encouraging us. The Psalm I quoted earlier, the twenty-third, makes it clear: The Lord is our shepherd.

Guilt and Fear?

In the past, we've sought to motivate people to accept Christ out of a sense of guilt or fear. Recognizing certain people are motivated by guilt and fear, leaders of many groups have used these motivations to move people to action. Particularly in a culture that was strongly Christian, where people understood as a part of a cultural pressure they should go to church, should be a Christian, should be compliant. This "in your face" approach was the beginning approach for many to lead people to accept Christ. A Christian might remind a person that they could be killed in a car wreck on the way home and then ask them if they had accepted Christ. If they were unsure about their response, the evangelist would remind them that, if they were killed in the car wreck, they would be certain to go to hell without being a committed Christian. That motivation may have worked in the past under other circumstances, but for very secular people today that motivation creates anger, frustration and sometimes strong rejection. The motivation for following Christ may be created by guilt for our misdeeds or our lack of responsibility. Certainly, guilt and fear do move us to be responsible in lots of ways, including everything from safe driving to having regular medical check-ups to paying our taxes on time. However, the positive motivation of realizing how great it is to follow Christ, the benefits, and the realization that Christianity works is much more effective in our contemporary culture.

Why We TELL

I cannot imagine anything more joyful, more powerful and more peaceful than serving God with my heart, mind, soul and body. I have over and over seen how following Christ created such powerful positive results for all. I have seen the power, dedication and prayer of the Korean Christians. While visiting the large Methodist Church in Seoul, I sat with literally thousands as they gathered for God's will. I've seen the vitality of these followers of Jesus in a determination to follow Jesus and make this world so much better. I have seen their evangelistic zeal. They are among the leaders in leading others to Christ. I have been to the mountains of Bolivia and joined in humble worship services in small mud brick churches as some of the poorest people on Earth joyfully sing praises to God. They are determined to follow Jesus no matter how difficult the economy is. I've watched those Bolivian Christians find vitality and joy even in difficult economic situations.

For 10 years, I was a part of starting churches in Russia. I preached before thousands. I watched former communists accept Jesus Christ as their Lord and Savior. We helped those people start churches, watched their enthusiasm and belief in the practical power of the way of Jesus Christ. I sat in meetings with former atheistic or agnostic communists in Russia and answered question after question as they wrestled with what was true and what was not true. I watched them make sense out of the way of Christ and become leaders in new churches. I sat with American businessmen at prayer meeting after prayer meeting as they discussed and shared about ethics and morality and integrity in the workplace and asked for God's guidance. I celebrated as families stood at the altar of the church and made their profession of faith to follow in the steps of Jesus. I watched a congregation grow from bitterness into great enthusiasm and joy as they came to believe that following Jesus Christ was the answer to the church and their personal lives. I saw countless people in the midst of real difficulty—difficulty of divorce or death, difficulty of economic struggle or family crisis, find in the teachings of Jesus a way to build a new life and a hope for the future.

In the following pages, we will review how to share our faith today in a secular American culture. With all the help you may find on these pages, the real key to your leading others to God's way is your own commitment.

My life, from the time that I was a young baby in the arms of my parents and brought to the altar of the church, has been dominated by the teachings of Jesus Christ. Like every Christian in

American society, I had a multitude of opportunities to abandon those ideals, criticize the church's failures and ridicule the hypocrites, but I found, even with our sins and faults, the Gospel of Jesus Christ works.

On one of the many trips I made to Russia, through a series of mistakes that were made, I was arrested and taken to be interrogated. As I sat, guarded by the Russian police, waiting for interrogation, I reflected upon all the stories I had heard about Christians living in the communist state, being asked to renounce their faith, to give up their convictions or be imprisoned, maybe killed. Those stories were real; they were part of the stories of torture and persecution that the Church went through in Communist Russia. As I sat, I thought, "Maybe that's what will be asked of me. Will I reject my faith? Will I reject what I was doing in Russia in order to be released? Will I give Christ Jesus up to keep from going to prison?" My decision in the chaos of that moment was no. I would stand my ground, no matter what I was asked. I would keep Christ's truth no matter what.

The interrogation was over quickly, as one of my Russian friends paid the bribe to the authorities and my brief imprisonment was over, and yet, I had made a decision in my mind: "The beliefs Jesus taught are true. I am His follower no matter what! I would not give it up, even for my life!" That's why we must share this good news.

Our motivation for sharing the Gospel with others should be the power of the Gospel itself, not just because we receive some kind of spiritual "brownie points" in the heavenly book of life. It is not just because sharing the Gospel will somehow cause our church to receive more contributions and grow. It is not just because sharing the Gospel will make our cantankerous friend a little nicer. We share Christ because being a Christian is so great. Being of Christ is so helpful. Being a follower of Christ is so truthful. Following Jesus' teachings is the key to peace on earth. The reason for sharing the Gospel is not to make ourselves more comfortable, more assured or more prosperous; it is because sharing the Gospel will help other people come to know the beautiful, powerful, helpful message and life of Jesus Christ. It is fantastic to be a Christian!

I was flying to a major city on the Gulf Coast where I was leading a workshop on evangelism. The plane was delayed in Atlanta, so we waited and eventually were able to leave. It was a small, crowded jet and my seat was near the front on the aisle. There were only two seats on each row and, as it was late and I had to speak the next morning, I hoped like everything that no one would be seated next to me. But as it happens most of the time, when we want to have an empty seat next to us it is filled. This time it was filled by a man who was bigger than the seat. He crowded into his seat and spilled over the armrest. His big muscular arm pushed into my seat. In the quiet that followed takeoff, he turned to me and said, "So, what do you do?" For any of us that is an interesting moment. For a pastor late at night, tired and wanting to rest, instead of seeing an opportunity to share the Gospel, I felt frustrated. I told him simply that I was a preacher, named the city I was going to, and said I was speaking the next day. Before he could ask me the second question I turned to him and asked, "What do you do?" He said with a smile on his face, "I'm the sheriff."

"Wow," I thought, "here's the sheriff and the evangelist on the airplane. What are we going to talk about?" We talked about everything—life in the south, hurricanes, the economy, law enforcement, the church and preaching. I asked him what the biggest problem in his county was. He paused for a moment and then with real tears in his eyes he began to describe the problems in his community. I said, "What do you mean, hurricanes and all the disasters have made people behave worse?" The sheriff then began to describe our human struggles. More than just wanting to make conversation, I really wanted to know what had happened, what was causing the problems. He turned to me with the same kind of authority he had when he was about to arrest someone for a crime, yet with tears in his eyes and said, "They don't have no Jesus. That's what's wrong."

The sheriff, in the midst of his sadness over the behavior of people in his county, realized that it was the teachings of Jesus that could give us the direction. It is the presence of God's power that can give us assurance. It is the teachings of Jesus that show us our self-esteem and purpose. We need Jesus Christ.

The sheriff's answer may seem simplistic. There are all kinds of factors in our society that create domestic abuse. There are all kinds of reasons why people behave in helpful and unhelpful ways. To simplify our needs in terms of Jesus Christ may seem an overstatement, but for those of us who have experienced the power of Christ, we know the simple answer of "They don't have no Jesus" reminds us of how powerful Jesus Christ is for each of us.

The purpose of this book is to solve that problem. I believe that Jesus Christ is God's answer to a struggling world that needs to know the truth. I have written this book out of the conviction that we need to know Jesus, and those of us who have found Christ in our lives have an obligation, a commission and an imperative to share. All of us need for the sheriff to look us in the eye and say that the problem in this world is, "They don't have no Jesus." You and I realize we can do something about that. While reading these pages I hope you and others will come to better know how to share the Gospel of Jesus Christ. May you remember the words of the sheriff, "They don't have no Jesus. That's what's wrong." May these words be your "orders" as they are mine.

Questions for Discussion and Personal Reflection

1. Begin with a time of prayer, thanking God for all He has done for you.
2. List all the benefits you have experienced by being a Christian.
3. Summarize in five words how great it is to be a Christian.
4. In three minutes, tell your story of making a commitment to Jesus Christ as Lord and Savior.
5. Sit alone in meditation and prayer and repeat the words of the sheriff.

Chapter 2
Effective

Choices

We love choices; we like to do whatever we want to do. We're proud of having a sense of freedom; we defend that right as part of our basic creative nature. And yet when we commit our lives to Christ, we give up some of that freedom in order to follow Jesus Christ. In Matthew 16:24 (NKJV), we are reminded by Jesus that if we are to be His followers: *"Whoever wants to be my disciple must deny themselves and take up their cross daily and follow me."* We need to take up our cross daily and follow Him. This calling of the disciples described in each of the gospels describes Jesus calling people to follow Him. Therefore, when Jesus commands us to love God with our heart, mind, soul and body, and love our neighbors as ourselves as described in Luke 10, we understand these are not only the Great Commandments but these are our instructions for living. It's not do them if you want or if you have time or if it's convenient, but do them! In Matthew 25:19–20, Jesus gives the Great Commission. It's the final instruction. In this commission, Jesus tells us to go make disciples. As we deal with the issue of sharing our faith and witnessing to others, we need to understand that we do this out of an understanding of how great it is to be a Christian and how clear Jesus was about telling us to share.

Evangelism is an imperative. Jesus didn't give us any choices. He simply told us to do it. As Jesus gathered on the hillside in Galilee, it was his final instructions. "Go make disciples!" was the last thing in His earthly form He told us to do.

My mother died in early April 2009. She and my dad had prepared well; they had a trust, a will. My dad had died several years before Mom. I was made the executor of the estate, being the oldest child. I had read the documents; I knew what to do and my brother, sister and I all understood and agreed. But, after Mother's death, when we were cleaning up her apartment, we found a handwritten, full-page document. It was a shock. My wife found it in the chest by her bed; she had written it out and entitled it, "My last will and testament." In it, she described things she wanted done, different than what was in the trust. There were no contradictions, just additional things. When we found it, I simply folded it up and put it in my pocket, deciding at that moment, we were not going to do this. Plans were already made; this was not necessary. Later that day, as we were sitting in the house, one of my five daughters who is a CPA was visiting with me at my desk. I thought she might be interested in the piece of paper, so I handed it to Jill and said, "Look what we found in Mom's apartment." Jill read it carefully and then said, "Dad, this is Grandma's last will and testament. She signed it." I explained to Jill we already had a trust and had already made arrangements and she said, "Dad, this is what she wanted done." When you have an accountant in the family, sometimes their determination to do things right makes things more complicated. I shook my head and stuffed the paper back in my pocket and then realized my daughter was right. I met with my brother and sister the next day; we did not want to do what my mother had asked, but we decided we had no choice. This is what she had asked; we were her children; we had to do what her last request was.

Since that day, I've thought a lot about Jesus' last instruction. Though sometimes we don't want to do evangelism; we're embarrassed, busy, unsure; we're afraid of the complications, the misunderstandings; we don't know for sure what to do and so we simply stuff it. Making disciples is what He told us to do. We, as followers of Jesus, His children, have no choice.

"I'm busy!"

Most of us are busy. Our world is filled with much stimulation; we have things to do and places to go. We want to be a part of the opportunities that are provided in so many ways by the world around us. So we fill our days with much to do. Pastors have responsibilities, obligations, tasks to do. There are church members in the hospital, sermons to write, newsletters to put together, air conditioners that don't work, toilets that are not working, members that need conversation and, consequently, it is easy to put evangelism at the bottom of the list. Jesus did not place it there; He made it an absolute order, instruction, responsibility. Certainly, in being honest about the task of sharing our faith with someone else, we must admit that it is sometimes difficult. Others may not want to listen, may not be interested, may be opposed to our ideas. We may not be good speakers, explainers, persuaders or even listeners. So the task is sometimes hard for us to do. Therefore, there are some basic steps to helping ourselves and our friends in the church to become people who can do evangelism. We need to help ourselves develop the skills to share the faith, be Christian witnesses effectively. The following are some simple steps.

1. It Is Your Job

The first is to understand it is part of the responsibility in being a Christian. It is our job. We have been instructed to make disciples, to share the Gospel. Whether we're tired, bashful, fearful or a little confused, the request is still the same. It's not to be difficult with ourselves, but it's just to understand this is what we are asked to do. The eight-year-old does not like to brush his teeth. It takes trouble, it's time-consuming, it tastes bad, it sometimes hurts. He's too busy. And yet, eventually as he grows older, he learns, whether it's convenient or not, he needs to brush his teeth. Evangelism is what we're supposed to be doing. Our ability to get the job of evangelism done is dependent, first, upon our clear decision that it's a priority. Among the thousands of priorities we have, evangelism is a major priority. Our task, with all of our reluctance, uncertainty and struggling with the issue, we must decide we're going to get it done. Our ability to make this happen, to follow any of the suggestions in this book, depends first upon our willing choice to do it.

My wife, Delia, is the chairman of an organization that had a series of projects that were put off, neglected, not getting done. So they created a "Git-R-Done" committee. Maybe in most churches, we need to create a "Git-R-Done" committee to get evangelism done, to get it organized, planned, carried out and celebrated. The task is clear: Git-R-Done!

2. It Works

Secondly, we must celebrate how wonderful it is to be a Christian, to remember the blessings, our privilege, our gratitude for what God has done for us in Jesus Christ, to be thankful for the joy, the help, and, most of all, our salvation and to celebrate that clearly in our own being by sharing this good news with other people. Because it is such profound good news, we need to find the words, the description, the vocabulary that expresses the joy and the power of the message of Jesus Christ that we have to share.

The second principle is celebrating not only how wonderful it is to be a Christian but how effective it is, how it works. Part of our decision to accomplish this is a confidence in what we're doing. The salesman that does not believe in the product is a poor salesman. The pastor who is unsure about the practicality of following Jesus is truly a hypocrite. The Christian that wants to do the job that God has given us needs to celebrate that it works, it makes a difference, it will change the world, it will bring peace on earth, it will give salvation for eternity, it will bring you eternal life. It works!

3. Be Prepared

The Boy Scouts have as their slogan, "Be Prepared." It's a pretty good idea. As a young boy, I was active in scouting; I loved the outdoors, loved the challenge of working through the ranks. But maybe the concept of being prepared was an idea that stuck most with me. We need to make a plan, schedule the meeting, plan the activities, follow through, double check on the details. This book is about planning, goals-setting, strategizing, assigning responsibilities, laying out a timetable, evaluating our task. These are all strategies that are a part of any good, healthy organization. Evangelism needs to be done in a healthy way. Too many times, we seek to satisfy the imperative by doing something for a moment and then forgetting about the rest of the task. It's easy to treat evangelism that way; have a one-Sunday emphasis on bringing a friend and then forget about it; celebrate the children who join the church through confirmation and don't mention it again until the next confirmation class; speak with your more evangelical church members in an affirming way about winning people to Christ and never do anything about it. Probably the most neglected aspect of any church's life is evangelism. This one of the priorities of Christ's teachings is set at the bottom of the list. We need to be prepared, plan carefully, work out the details and reprove the people. This book is about being prepared.

4. Pay Attention

In school, one of the things that teachers said most often to me was "Pay attention!" It's so easy to get distracted. My natural hyperactivity took me off on a multitude of tangents no matter what the teacher was trying to emphasize. One of the problems that we have in doing evangelism is that we don't pay attention. There are some factors that are priorities for us to pay attention to. First, we need to pay attention to the people that we're trying to share the

faith with. In the sections on individual witnessing, the emphasis
must be listening to our friends, knowing what the situation is, all
the way through our four-step TELL process. So often the arrogance of our witnessing is based upon our refusal to pay real attention to the person we're trying to lead to Christ. They've gone
through struggles and had problems, faced difficulties and have real
needs. The key to the Christian faith is to be like the Good Samaritan and notice the needs; listen to your friend, pay attention to the
member of your family, understand where your fellow employee is
hurting. And, it's out of that sensitivity that you'll be effective in
leading them to Christ.

Significant changes have happened in our society; the value system and faith emphasis have radically changed. Christianity is no
longer the dominant force in our society. It is easy for a committed
Christian to reject so many of the facts, values and actions of our
secular friends as simply wrong without ever attempting to understand what's going on, why they're happening, what their needs are,
what the values that are being presented are. It's time for us to scold
ourselves, wake ourselves up, remind ourselves to pay attention.
Paying attention is not only paying attention to the individuals
around that we seek to witness to but it's to pay attention to what's
happening in our culture, to understand the trends, to understand
the major problems, to understand the factors that are influencing
the way we behave and communicate, to understand the pressures
that are upon families and individuals. The simplistic idea of
accepting Christ seems so naïve when it's being suggested to an
individual whose life is packed full of problems and issues and crises. The church needs to pay attention.

Another way that evangelism needs to be done is responding to
the needs, just as Jesus did. In the fourth chapter of Luke, Jesus
describes that He came to *"proclaim freedom for the prisoners and recovery
of sight for the blind, to release the oppressed, to proclaim the year of the Lord's
favor"* (v. 18–19). We need to be like Jesus; that is, affirm that we are

listening to the hurts of our society and we want to help. This is not some fake kind of way of trying to convince others of our genuineness; it is our genuineness. It is what it means to be a Christian. We are concerned about what's going on, where the hurts are, where the needs are.

5. Meet Needs

This desire to help, this commitment to make a difference, is basic to being a Christian. When Jesus describes in the twenty-fifth chapter of Matthew those who will be received in heaven and those who won't, the answer is simple: it's those who responded to the needs of others. " *'For I was hungry and you gave me something to eat, I was thirsty and you gave me something to drink, I was a stranger and you invited me in, I needed clothes and you clothed me, I was sick and you looked after me, I was in prison and you came to visit me...whatever you did for one of the least of these brothers of mine, you did for me'* " (Matthew 25:35–36, 40).

Jesus' teachings are clear in terms of our call to compassion, care and noticing the hurts and needs around us. But it's not simply the act of noticing the matters; it's the act of doing. He tells the story of the Good Samaritan and finishes the story by telling us to do the same thing. These teachings are clear. We're called to pay attention; but, more than pay attention, to do something about it. It is by that act of noticing the needs that the effectiveness of our ministries will be clear. To respond to the needs is a directive for prayer and sermons and for planning classes of Christian education and Bible Study; it's a directive for the programs of a local church and a church denomination, and it becomes the means by which we graphically show the non-Christian the power of Jesus Christ. Jesus healed the sick, cared for the hungry, dealt with the hurting, so we are called to do the same. Half of our society suffer from chronic depression; more than half the marriages in America end in divorce;

loneliness, lack of communication skills, the problems of inappropriate behavior and unkind actions are continually the detriment of our society and our individual behavior. We are called to help, to stand up for human justice, human rights, human needs and human hurts.

6. Prayer

Prayer is an important part of our sharing the Gospel. For us to be transformed and empowered, we need the Spirit of God to guide, direct, inspire and encourage. Prayer is a way in which we become more aware of God's presence. Whether it's prayer in a group or alone; whether it's prayer on the way to talk to a friend or alone in our room, prayer is a way that we connect with power, insight, understanding and set our mind in the right spiritual direction to be able to share the good news. To pray for the person we want to talk to, to pray for ourselves, that we'll say the right words, to pray for our preparation, that we will listen well, to pray for our vision, that we'll be clear. Prayer is important!

7. Team Work

We need the support of others. The encouragement, the accountability and the partnership—this is what the Church is for; we need to ask our Sunday school class, prayer group, mission team and other friends at church to pray for us as we seek to share our faith with others. We need the encouragement, the instruction and the correction of good friends in the faith. The community of the followers of Jesus Christ provides us that support. We do not need to do this alone. Not only is God with us, but our Christian friends are with us as well. Their help is not only in terms of encouragement and affirmation, but it's also in terms of coaching, correction, planning. We need to build a network of friends to help us to share our faith better. All of us know people who compete in athletic events; many of us have been competitors ourselves and we understand that in order to compete well, we need to practice, we need to learn, we need the help of others in preparation. One of my daughters runs in marathons and, in order to do that, she has to prepare well, use the help of her friends, know what needs to be done, eat well and sleep well in order to enter into the marathon. My grandsons play football and to play football well, you have to practice, work out with the team and spend time learning the plays and skills in order to compete and win. It's not only sports, but every aspect of life involves preparation. So it is with sharing our faith.

8. Trust God

In the prayer that Jesus gave us, he affirms God's kingdom will come, on earth as it is in heaven. The benediction that we place on the end of the Lord's Prayer is simply, *"For thine is the kingdom, the power, and the glory forever."* The prayer found in Matthew's gospel in the sixth chapter provides for us an understanding of our trust in God, that God's kingdom will come, that God's will shall be done. In doing evangelism, we need to trust that God is active in this world. In the Sermon on the Mount, Jesus tells us to ask and we will receive, knock and it will be opened unto us. In the seventh chapter of Matthew, these promises are made clearly. Then why is it that we don't trust that God is in the act of evangelism? The Great Commission is God's will; we need to trust that what happens will be God's will. Certainly, He has given us free will to make a choice to say no to hope, to possibilities, to new life in Christ. We understand that every individual has that privilege and God will not take away our free will, and, yet, God influences, works, acts to lead us to the truth. He gives us the conviction that His will shall be done, that people will be led to Christ, that the world will follow the way of Christ's teachings on love, that human beings will be responsible, that the truth will be told, that His will shall be done. The importance of understanding this last principle is that we need to trust. We continually think that it's totally up to us, that we have to do it all by ourselves. We become anxious, frustrated; we tend to become manipulators more easily; we don't trust that God will use what we've done in the best way possible.

As we were holding meetings and rallies all across Russia to establish protestant churches and proclaim the Gospel of Jesus Christ; as we were speaking to crowds of people and having wonderful positive results, it was one of the smallest of all meetings, a little gathering in a library in Voronezh, Russia. Outside the library was a giant statue of Lenin, and inside the library were a handful of Christians from Oklahoma conducting a meeting to explain Christianity and ask people to follow Jesus. We were excited to make the witness in any way possible, and yet, discouraged that so few came. Our translator, Irina, translated the sermon well and spoke to the Russian people clearly and, as the last prayer was given, she translated the words of the prayer. There were interests and good questions, but there seemed to be no results. Nothing happened, except that this English teacher at Voronezh State University, who had gotten the job as our translator, as she translated the message, gave her own life to Jesus Christ. At the same time that God was calling her to follow Jesus, God was asking her to be a pastor. She said yes to both. Nobody on the team had thought to talk to the translator about Jesus; nobody on the team had imagined that one of the best teachers in the whole community was the lady who had been with us all along, translating every word that we said. If we could have chosen the key person in the Voronezh community to follow Jesus Christ, logic would have told us to pick Irina, but, in our busy-ness, we looked and looked for others. Today, Irina is pastor of one of the most thriving churches in Russia. She's the deeply committed leader of the church in Russia.

Sometimes, we need to let God bring the fruit. I grew up in a farming community; my first two churches were in the Wheat Belt across Oklahoma. As hard as a farmer tries, planting the wheat just right, cultivating it properly, fertilizing—doing all the right farming, it is not the US government, the local farmer's co-op, nor the owner of the land where the wheat has been planted, who causes the seed to germinate and the plant to grow. It is God who causes the wheat to develop so the harvest can be done. We need to pray and trust.

Questions for Discussion and Personal Reflection

1. How would you describe witnessing or sharing the faith?
2. Are there stories that you could share about how you have been able to witness effectively and successfully?
3. Are there stories that you would share where you really messed up an opportunity to share the faith?
4. As you begin to read these pages on sharing the faith, if you had to use the letters T-E-L-L as a description of sharing the faith, how would you do that? What characteristic begins with T, E, L and L?
5. Spend some time in prayer that you might become a living evangelist.

Chapter 3
Need to Know the Territory

Meredith Wilson's *Music Man* is a fun story of a travelling salesman. There's a song in the beginning of the musical where the whole group of travelling salesmen on a railroad train sing, "You've Got to Know the Territory." It may seem like a silly song, but it is a profound reality. Anyone who has been a travelling salesman knows you need to know what the needs of your customers are. Anyone who has tried to compete in the marketplace of life knows you've got to meet the needs of the client, the customer, the patron. Industries, small businesses and professionals all learn that you've got to know the territory. You've got to know about the people that you're dealing with, sharing with, selling to, serving, helping. So it is with witnessing to the faith. So many times in our enthusiasm to share the good news of Jesus Christ, we do not take time to try to understand those who we are communicating with and, consequently, we become arrogant, sometimes obnoxious, often irrelevant and sometimes just comical. Today, Christians need to understand those that they want to share with. To share Christ with a family member or friend we need to listen and try to understand. Christians need to understand the non-Christian community, the culture, the values, the premises, the questions. One of the first steps in understanding is to listen.

Listen

Bill knew that his coworker Charlie never went to church. On Monday morning when Bill spoke about things at church, Charlie never responded with a positive word. Eventually, Charlie shared some stories that let Bill know that he didn't go to church, that he'd had some bad experiences as a kid and was determined not to go back to church again. As they became closer associates and partners for the construction job that they were doing, they found that they knew each other better and better and became closer and closer friends. Bill so much wanted Charlie to know the good news that he knew so well. Charlie was angry about a lot of things, bewildered about the way that things had happened in his own life, the way he had been treated by his stepfather. Bill wanted Charlie to understand what Jesus could mean; he wanted Charlie to understand the power of prayer and experience the joy of being with other Christians who would be supportive and helpful. When Charlie's marriage began to fall apart, Bill tried to be as understanding as he could. His church was holding a divorce ministry program and he invited Charlie to the program and, though Bill was not divorced, he went with Charlie to the classes. The people in the classes were hurting, but the leaders cared so much about Charlie. This was for Charlie the worst time in his life. He found such support that his attitude began to soften for church and for God. Bill realized that he needed to tell Charlie more about Christ. He needed to tell Charlie what the church was all about and about Jesus. And yet, he was so hesitant; he knew how much Charlie had been hurt as a kid and how much Charlie was going through now and so Bill just listened. For hours, he and Charlie talked. Bill took the time to try to understand what Charlie had gone through and been though and what his fears were about the church. When the day came when Charlie asked Bill a few simple questions about God and prayer the door was open. As they sat together that evening on the front porch of Bill's house, Bill knew this was the time. He realized all the listening he had done for all of those months, all the compassion that he had shared and all the friendship he and Charlie had came together as they talked that night. Bill had listened well. He didn't need to argue with Charlie; he just shared, and, in the sharing, Charlie's life was changed. Charlie made a decision to put aside all of anger and the fears of what had happened as a child. In the midst of the most hurtful time in his life, he asked God to help him. In the quietness of that evening on the porch, Charlie prayed for the first time since his childhood. Part of the reason that happened was because Bill had listened so well.

So it is with all of us. We need to know the territory, know what's going on and understand our friends. Part of this is to understand the culture of our society, the language, the criticisms of the church and the value systems that have changed. In order to share, we've got to listen and we've got to pay attention. That is, not only to pay attention to what's being said but to pay attention to the changes, the language, the vocabulary, the situation and be able to speak in a spirit of understanding. One of the realities is that so many people who might be ambiguous about the church are so simply because they haven't heard; they don't know much about the church. They don't know what the church is doing or why the church is doing it. The culture is not strongly Christian as it once was; much of the vocabulary and stories used to explain the faith are simply not understood. We need to listen to our friends and acquaintances so that we know where they are, what they understand and what they don't understand.

Jane had developed a very close friendship with Ann Marie as they worked together in the secretarial pool at the insurance company. They had lunch together often and talked about all kinds of things. Ann Marie had not had any experience in the church for at least the last 10 years. Growing up, it had been marginal; she had visited several different churches, but never was involved in one. So, when they began to talk about church one day and her friend Jane invited her to church, Ann Marie was filled with questions. The conversation centered on answering all kinds of questions about what Christians believe, what they do and how they worship. Ann Marie was not ready to have anything to do with a church unless she understood what it was all about. Eventually, she became an active part of the Christian faith and a deeply devout Christian, but it was only because Jane was patient and took the time to explain the answers to so many questions.

Demographics

We need to know the territory. Much of what we need to know is not just what we need to know as individuals but as the church itself. If the church seeks to minister to people within the community, it needs to understand what's going on with the community, what the hurts are, what the pains are, what the needs are and what the demographics are. If the church is to be, as Jesus instructed, like the Good Samaritan, we need to be ready to help wherever the needs are. Consequently, we need to know what those needs and problems are. Churches need to do demographic studies of their community so as to be sensitive to the needs that exist within their communities and respond to those needs as Jesus instructed. Churches need to understand the impact of various changes and be responsive to the hurts within the community. The church needs to know the territory, listen and pay attention to the place where the church has been called by God to serve.

I've helped many churches do demographic studies of their neighborhood and community. Oftentimes, a church that has been at one particular site for a long time, and in restudying their neighborhood, they find that there are major changes happening that the church members were simply not aware of. Oftentimes, church members, over the years, have moved out of the neighborhood where their home church is and yet they still drive back to the church to attend, thinking that everything in the neighborhood is as it was when they lived there.

Once, I worked with a church that did a demographic study of their neighborhood and found, to their surprise, that the neighborhood was not a neighborhood of retired people, as the predominantly retired people congregation thought, but the neighborhood had changed. New, young families had moved in and it was predominantly a young family neighborhood, as it had once been when many of the members joined many years ago. The congregation began a new program for children, and opened a daycare center, and the church, in ministering to the neighborhood, changed, grew and found new vitality. We need to pay attention; we need to know what's happening in our neighborhoods.

Cultural Shift

All of us realize that things change. Culture changes; it has changed in everyone's lifetime. Things are different than they were when you were a child or even what they were like 10 years ago. In American society, culture has significantly changed and shifted. We need to know about the changes and shifts. Oftentimes, our local church becomes a kind of ghetto of ideas. We think everyone is like us. Or, at least, everyone we associate with is like us, and we don't realize that the vast number of people who need to know Christ are a part of a culture that is quite different from the one with which we are familiar. We need to understand what's changed in our society: values of family, marriage, work, business, technology. Simple things having to do with change like music and ways of communicating are critical in reaching new people for Christ.

Radical shifts in the Church's place in a culture have changed significantly. Dan Kimball explains:

> *We are living in an increasingly "post-Christian" culture. America once was more of a "Christian nation" whose influences and values were aligned with Judeo-Christian values and ethics. Even most atheists had a good sense of the story line of the Bible and its main characters, and usually respected the Bible and Christian pastors. Movies and media generally taught values and ethics that aligned for the most part with the Bible.*
>
> *However, the world around us has drastically changed over the past 30 years or so. In our increasingly post-Christian culture, the influences and values shaping emerging generations are no longer aligned with Christianity* (Kimball, p. 15).

A particular church decided to use its newsletter as a way of reaching new people. They sought to get names and addresses from countless places to send their weekly newsletter, and, in the course of their study, they came to realize how important social networking, the internet, emails and Facebook were. With the help of several new members of their church, they began to look at communicating through the new media in our society. They built a beautiful webpage for the church; the congregation was on Facebook; the pastor mentioned aspects of social networking in sermons, and soon, the church began to relate more to a whole generation of their community, just by changing the means of communication and some vocabulary.

We need to know what's going on with the different age in our communities. How people of different ages are communicating, living, talking and believing today. This is sometimes known as "generational theory." It is easy to be aware of the difference in generations; old people, young people and middle-aged people seem to be different. We've talked about boomers and Gen X throughout our society and we're aware of the differences in generation. And, yet, we need to study those differences more carefully. Generational theory has helped us to realize that the way that we're raised and the environmental situations that have happened in our growing up period and in our life have influenced our lifestyle. Consequently, our society is not made up of one culture but many generational cultures. If we want to reach people who are deeply involved in their generational culture, we need to learn the vocabulary, the situation, the feelings, the hopes, dreams and prejudices of that generation. Different sociologists vary in their way of dividing American culture into different generations. Generally speaking, the division is the "Greatest Generation," those who grew up in the Great Depression, the "Silent Generation," those who were born during the Great Depression or WWI, the Baby Boomers, who were born from 1946 to 1964 following WWII, Generation X, those born from the 1960s to the late 1970s, the Millennial or Generation Y, those born from the mid-1970s to the early 2000s and Generation Z, those born from the early 1990s to the late 2000s. It's important that we understand the generations in our congregation and the generations that we're seeking to reach for Christ. Vocabulary, goals, expectations and behavioral patterns are influenced heavily by generational emphases.

Amy was a member of the evangelism committee of her church. They decided to put a major focus upon encouraging each member of the church to share their faith. It was a big challenge; doing personal witnessing or sharing is hard to do today, particularly when it's done across generational lines. But, Amy, with her enthusiasm for Christ, was determined that she was going to share her faith wherever. She worked for a small business; she had become the head of the advertising department in that business. The owner was a really caring, gentle guy that she loved to work for—until she began to share her faith with him as they worked on the projects for the company. He hadn't been to church in years; he was a moral guy, responsible, in his early seventies. He was interested in getting back to church, and, when she told him about the excitement of her congregation and her own excitement and commitment to Christ, he began to ask some questions. She responded back, but found that her answers didn't seem to click with him. He was of the Silent generation, and she was a Millennial. When they talked about business matters, they could communicate, but when they talked about faith, it was as if they lived on different planets. She became frustrated and struggled trying to think how she could explain to him what Christ meant with all of his legalistic understandings of religion and faith; his vocabulary that was so different from hers. She admired him; she was glad she was working for him; she wanted him to know Christ as she did. But she had to learn and listen and try to understand before she ever was really effective in leading him back to church.

45

Generational differences make a difference and we need to know the territory and how to communicate. The story of Amy and her boss is a simple illustration of our need to understand the people with whom we seek to share Christ. It's like understanding a person from a different country. People within our own culture who are of different generations have different experiences, histories, language and illustrations, so, to explain Christ, we need to seek to understand. Most of the time, that means we need to listen carefully. In listening, we need to seek to understand. For years, psychologists have taught us that we are the product of our environment–things that happen to us and in our culture, disease of our family–our experiences in life influence how we speak and translate or understand how others speak to us. It's important to realize that our generational differences are real and, if we are going to share the faith, we need to learn how to speak about Christ in the different worlds of the different generations.

Systems

Much has been done in recent years by sociologists and organizational development researchers on the importance of systems. The research began in studying families, realizing that there were certain family systems that created phenomena within the family, behavioral patterns that were passed on. We began to realize that there were family systems in churches and businesses. Organizations develop systems of doing things and those systems become critical in understanding how people believe, act and participate. So it is as we seek to share our faith with our friends and families, we need to understand the systems.

Joel worked for a particular industry that had been fairly successful; he had worked for them for 10 years. His church made a major emphasis upon reaching people for Christ. On that Sunday morning they began the program he signed the covenant that he would begin to be more of a witness for Jesus in all of his life. He did not realize the implications of this for his company. In the weeks that followed that emphasis on personal witnessing in his church, he had thought about how to witness effectively. He had many close friends, many people that were active in the company who did not have any church. As far as he knew, they were not Christians in any kind of form or fashion, and he wanted to share the faith with them. There were particular ways that the company did things that seemed strange and, often, very difficult to deal with. Yet, now as a new active Christian witness, Joel did not realize how much trouble he was in. The CEO of the company who had created the company years before dominated the way that so many things were done. Joel found out that the CEO had had some pretty bad experiences with the church as a child and he had decided in his adult life that he simply would not have anything to do with faith or church, except on a very personal basis for himself. It worked fine until Joel became very active, inviting and encouraging in the company. Another characteristic of the company was that the CEO wanted to micromanage everything. He had done this since Joel had worked there and everyone had learned to work with corporate management, knowing that they were going to make rules and guidelines for every single thing. It sometimes became dysfunctional and oftentimes was frustrating and yet, because the company still did well, nothing changed. Until Joel became active in sharing the faith and the CEO found out about it. He became frustrated, angry, bewildered; he couldn't directly deal with Joel and yet he could indirectly. Joel felt himself pressured, accused, bewildered. After going through all kinds of struggles, Joel realized that he should have thought about how the company operated, about the boss and what his feelings were. He realized he could have witnessed in a lot of other ways that wouldn't have been so difficult for the company to handle.

This story helps us see that we must understand the environment and system if we're really to be effective in sharing the faith and leading people to Christ. It is not that we have to become expert sociologists and group behavioral geniuses; we simply need to realize, in Joel's case, that the CEO didn't care for the church and that he micromanaged everything in the company. If Joel had thought about this before, things would have worked better. He would have witnessed differently, and it would have been more effective.

In our eagerness to tell the world about how glorious it is to be a Christian, sometimes we make mistakes because we don't "know the territory;" we don't listen to our friends and understand what makes them tick and where they hurt and what the influences in their lives are. We don't pay attention to the systems that are operating in our families, businesses and even churches. We don't pay attention to the generational differences that influence us so strongly. The cultural changes seem to bewilder us; yet, we must listen, pay attention. Demographics are a scientific way of dealing with the shifts and changes. We need to use every method possible to do a better job for God.

Paul says in First Corinthians 9:22, *"I have become all things to all people so that by all possible means I might save some."* The paragraph in which this sentence is found describes Paul's desire to do anything that is necessary to lead someone to Christ. This may be sometimes hard for us to understand and yet the emphasis is clear: we need to do what's necessary to lead people to Christ. To know the territory or to understand people is one of the most basic things necessary for us to be able to share the faith. Unless we really understand the individuals, circumstances, situation, culture, demographics, system, we will not be effective. It's not some manipulative idea that we just want to understand in order to say the right words; it's based upon the premise that Jesus taught, that we're to love our neighbors as ourselves. In 1 Corinthians 9, Paul gives us this instruction to do whatever is necessary, but the understanding of doing what's necessary is found a few chapters later when he tells the church at Corinth that *"Love is patient, love is kind. It does not envy, it does not boast, it is not proud. It is not rude, it is not self-seeking, it is not easily angered, it keeps no record of wrongs.*

Love does not delight in evil but rejoices with the truth." From this description, we realize that we do the things necessary in the context of love to lead someone to Christ.

Questions for Discussion and Personal Reflection

1. Consider the various topics of knowing the territory mentioned in this chapter. Discuss listening, demographics, cultural shift and systems as a way of reviewing the factors within our communities.
2. Describe your experience realizing factors about individuals or the community or organizations as you have sought to work with, persuade, influence or survive in those organizations.
3. Consider your sharing of the faith with some of the persons you know who are quite different. What would you need to know in order to do the best job of sharing the faith?
4. In this chapter in the book, we've reviewed some ways to understand the territory. What are some other words or ways that you would use to describe differences among individuals, groups and within our communities where we're sharing the faith?
5. What are some dangers or things to be careful about in speaking to others about Christ?
6. Consider the times that you or others have been really successful in leading someone to Christ; what did you do? What were the characteristics of understanding that were present and practiced?
7. Spend some moments in prayer, praying for the different groups within your community that you would be able to witness in those various groups.

Chapter 4
Fishing

A story is told in Matthew 4:18–22 and Luke 5:1–11 where Jesus says to some fishermen, *"Come, follow me and I will make you fishers of men."* Immediately they left their nets and followed Him. The implication of this is so simple. The job of a Christian is to fish for people, to catch them and lead them to Christ. The metaphor Jesus used was direct and to the point. We understand catching fish, bait, nets and contemporary fishing gear. We understand something about fishing. We need to find the meaning of the metaphor. In the story Jesus says several important things for us to understand. These principles of evangelism are made clear in the resurrection and ascension experience when Jesus tells us to go make disciples of everyone and teach them the things that He taught. The fishing metaphor can be very helpful for the Christian.

As biblical narratives tell the story of Jesus we realize the image of fishing becomes a metaphor that first century Christians could identify with clearly. The men to whom Jesus spoke on the lake were fishermen. The people he dealt with in Galilee understood fishing. Even the sophisticated urbanites in Jerusalem knew about fishing. It was a metaphor that was understandable and usable.

The fishing metaphor still has significant meaning. Fishing today is usually for recreation instead of a life source; although it's not an everyday practice, we know about fishing, bait, casting the net, casting the line.

We understand about searching for the fishing hole, the well stocked pond, the fast moving trout stream. We understand about fishing where the fish are. We also understand that there is a skill to fishing. We need to know how to prepare the bait, how to cast the line, how to bring in the catch, how to fish so we catch fish. In the end, the purpose of fishing is not just the enjoyment of doing it, it is to catch fish.

The Goal of Fishing Is to Catch Fish

Probably the difference in the metaphor between the first century and the 21st century is that during the first century it was an absolute necessity to catch lots of fish. In the 21st century, fishing has become recreation. For many it is a family event, a fun time and a source of relaxation. In biblical times fishing was not recreation, it was vocation. Maybe we have forgotten what fishing really is. It is about producing results. The metaphor of becoming fishers of people that Jesus illustrated was a metaphor about getting results. It is the same way with evangelism, leading people to Christ. We have forgotten the purpose of all this is to allow new people to come to know the wonderful joy of following Jesus, the power and vitality of Holy Spirit. It is about results, not simply having an evangelism campaign. It is helping people find the joy and power of Christianity, not about the number of teams going out and witnessing in the neighborhood. It is about how many people come to Christ and His church, not about your new evangelism slogan or witness speech. It is about a secular person changing and committing his or her life to Christ!

After Jesus had spoken the words *"Come, follow me and I will make you fishers of men"* (Matthew 4:19), the fishermen became a part of the family. *"So they pulled their boats up on shore, left everything and followed Him"* (Luke 5:11). The model for witnessing is not only inviting people, it is becoming involved, building a relationship and following Jesus. The important aspect of the story that is often missed is that these fishermen joined the community. They didn't just come and meet Jesus, or affirm Jesus, or praise Jesus; they became the church, the followers, the family.

Fishing is to lead a person to make a commitment not only to follow Christ, but to become part of the Jesus movement. Fishing is to catch fish that will stay caught, not the ones that are thrown back after the fisherman has had the fun of catching them. It is the full experience.

The call that Jesus makes upon us all is the call to become fishers of people, which means basic steps that are a part of basic fishing. They are as follows: first, decide; take the time, the energy and go fishing. Second, prepare, do whatever is needed to catch fish. Third, practice, know what you are doing. Fourth, find where the fish are and go to where they are. Fifth, do the act; cast the line or the net. Sixth, bring in the fish. Some fishermen might call it land the fish. Finally, keep the fish.

To put these steps into contemporary practical goals: Decide to do evangelism, prepare to do evangelism, do evangelism where non-Christian people are and be well prepared in the deed of evangelism. Bring new people to church, to Christ, help them make a decision to stay and support them in their decision to stay. Put the new Christian to work for Christ!

The biggest issue in evangelism in the church today is that we seem to be reluctant to do it. There are so many things to do. We can get involved in the community, we can have fellowship, we can devise and develop wonderful worship services, we can have spiritual life retreats and keep ourselves busy in good ways. We seem to be too busy to lead others to Christ.

Do What He Told You to Do

The sad thing about this reality is that evangelism is the last thing Jesus asked us to do. It is his final instruction. It is called the Great Commission (Matthew 28:16–20). The scene described in Matthew's gospel is the scene of Jesus meeting His disciples on the

Mount of Olives after the resurrection. They were standing around talking and when they saw Jesus they worshipped Him. Jesus explained that He was going to leave. The picture is magnificent and has been made famous by artists over the centuries. It is a simple story of Jesus giving his final instruction, *"Therefore go and make disciples of all nations"* (Matthew 28:19). Why are we so reluctant?

When Jesus' disciples gathered on the Mount of Olives they were in the midst of a terrible, difficult transition. Jesus had been killed. Yet there He was, resurrected! He joined them, talked with them, touched them and now He was giving them instructions. His last instruction was for His disciples to go into the entire world, preach the Gospel and teach the world what He had taught them. I can imagine the disciples had many different ideas about what they were going to do. Some thought they would go back to fishing. Some thought they would create new alliances with other revolutionary groups. I think we can tell from the biblical narrative that most of them were ready to give up and quit. Yet, it was only a few days later when they met in the upper room in Jerusalem (Acts 1 & 2). Luke described what happened to them as tongues of fire, a mighty wind. More amazing than Luke's flowery language was what happened. They went out on the streets of Jerusalem on the day of Pentecost and thousands were led to Christ. The church began and increased significantly. Theologians have described it in so many ways. It was the power of the Holy Spirit, the call of God, the willingness of the disciples.

To put it bluntly they decided to do what He told them. They decided to follow the instruction given them by their Lord and Savior Jesus on the Mount of Olives. The Great Commission is simply doing what He told us to do: make disciples. The questions about shall we be witnesses, shall we tell the story, shall we lead people to Christ are really moot when you consider what it means to accept Jesus as Lord and Savior. If He is our Lord; He is our leader, our boss and we are to do what He said. This book isn't about a compromise or a new plan; it is simply doing what He told us to do.

For us to teach to our fellow Christians what it means to be a witness and how to tell our story, we must begin with a decision that we are going to do what He told us to do. Jesus was about commitment. He pulled no punches. He told us if we are going to be His disciples we will have to take up our cross and follow Him (Mark 8:34). Not follow Him some of the time, when it is convenient or when it's easy, but follow Him all the time.

Evangelism is not just something that churches do when they need more contributors to pay off a building debt; it is not something that churches do every year at Easter when the confirmation class finishes its work and young people stand in front of the congregation to make their profession of faith. Evangelism is what we are about! The question is not about our respecting or not respecting other points of view and other religions, nonbelievers or atheists, evangelism is respectfully seeking to lead all of them to Christ. Evangelism is doing what He told us to do: Go fish!

Jack was a really tough guy. He looked that way. Somehow, expressions on his face, his muscular build and his shaved head made him look extra strong, even a little repulsive at times. You had a feeling in just looking at him that he was ready to do some kind of violence to you or to someone else. And yet, his looks were quite the opposite of what kind of person he was; Jack was gentle and loving. He was kind in every kind of circumstances. His life was one dedicated to helping other people. He wanted to make things better.

Jack hadn't always been this way; as a young boy, he had had problems. School was difficult. Because of his learning disabilities, he had been at the bottom of the class and seen early as a trouble maker when there were difficulties. If a group was creating problems, Jack was usually accused of being part of the group. But, inside the mix of values and harsh lifestyle, Jack was struggling with what was right. They closed down his school; kids were transferred to different

schools in their neighborhoods and Jack found himself with a new
school, a new group of kids and he could start over again. He was
befriended by two guys that were active in the local church youth
group. Jack went; he heard the stories of faith and truth that he had
never heard before. He became acquainted with Christ on a first person kind of basis, not because someone told him about Christ but
because he read it for himself. And what he read in the New Testament he was very impressed by. Even as a 14-year-old boy, he became
articulate in understanding what Christ taught. He turned his life
around, overcame some learning disabilities and began to do well in
school. By the time he graduated, he had been elected as president of
his high school senior class. In the years that followed, in Jack's vocational choices, marriage, children, his commitment to follow Christ
became the driving force. The lessons that he had learned the hard
way became lessons that helped him share with other people who
were struggling with life, values and difficulties. Jack became the
friend of those in need, the rescuer of people in trouble and the
spokesman for what was right and loving and caring in his community. People came to know this man and his example of being a
Christian. He became a leader in inviting others to follow Christ as
well. Because of his clear commitment, his motivation was without
question. As the culture changed, Jack learned to tell the story of
Christ in a slightly different way. As circumstances were different and
people he met had different experiences and lifestyles, Jack learned
how to explain Christ in a way that was appropriate for them. He led
others to Christ. It was at the annual state meeting of his denomination and they were giving out awards, that Jack was shocked, surprised and emotionally affirmed as he was given an award for his
evangelism. They called it the "Jesus Award." It was simple; they said
it was the award for doing what Jesus taught. The plaque they gave
him hangs on the wall of his shop. The plaque represents the truth
about a man who was committed to leading people to Christ.

Jack is truly an evangelist. He is an example and a leader. He is doing simply what Jesus asked.

The story of Jack is told here to help us understand that evangelists are ordinary people who go through ordinary struggles. The old model of an evangelist standing on the street corner with Bible in hand, preaching to people passing by is simply not a model that works today. Evangelists are ordinary, hardworking people who have gone through significant changes in their own lives and have come to share the story of Jesus Christ with their friends.

Passion With Purpose

The problem with the fishing metaphor is that without passion it isn't more than a simple word picture. If you don't care anything about fishing and find it unpleasant, dirty, unrewarding and smelly, fishing is a poor metaphor. Fishing for fish or human beings is not a good idea unless you love it. The keys to evangelism are to love it and have passion for it. We can't be evangelistic because we are told to, or because someone cons us into it, or because someone teaches us a formula of words to ask someone else. We are evangelistic because we want to be, because we believe in the Gospel of Jesus Christ, because we know it is the best thing in our lives, because we know the kingdom of God will change the world, because we believe the future of humanity depends upon the teachings of Jesus Christ, because we know what a difference it is to be caught and brought to Jesus. It means everything to us because we have experienced it. The fishing Jesus speaks about in the story of the fishermen is fishing that takes all the priority. It has to do with something you would rather do than go anyplace else or do anything else; it is what you know is satisfying, needed, helpful, refreshing and empowering. To consider how you can personally lead people to follow Jesus has to do with your own commitment. The passion of evangelism and Christian fishing comes out of commitment to Christ. For a church leader to teach their congregation how to share or witness, the congregation first must care. They must want to lead people to Christ. They must believe it is the best thing they can do. I am asking you to consider "fishing" as Jesus calls it, the most important thing we can do.

Passion with purpose makes evangelism easy. Passion with purpose empowers the most reluctant, bashful individual to be able to tell someone else about what Jesus means to them. Passion with purpose is what helps a congregation organize in order to develop an effective, workable evangelism program.

The local church was having the first meeting of the new year with their evangelism committee. The nominating committee had selected good people to be on this committee including people who everyone felt really cared about reaching new people for Christ, salvation, the church and Jesus Christ. So they began to discuss how to share the faith and how to reach new people. The more they talked the more the conversation turned to negatives, criticisms, griping about all kinds of things. The meeting eventually ended and everyone went home vowing in their minds to never return to that committee. It wasn't fun, satisfying or empowering. The question the pastor had once the meeting was over and in the days that followed was simple. How could he instill passion in the minds of the evangelism committee, the whole church and even himself?

Our Goal

At the sales meeting at the local automobile dealership the new sales manager gave a little pep talk about how to sell cars, how important it was, etc. When he finished he put a chart on the wall displaying the goals for each employee, how many cars they needed to sell. Unless they met those criteria they may be looking for another job. As Bill listened to the talks and heard the description, he became furious about the idea of a goal, the idea that someone was saying he had to perform in a certain way or he would be fired. He wanted to quit that day. He thought he was a good salesman but he didn't want to work because he was given a set of instructions and goals. That evening when he sat down at the dinner table his wife Beverly told him so sweetly, so beautifully! It was like everything in his life changed as she said, "I'm pregnant." Then she told him approximately the due date. He sat there excited, overjoyed, proud and scared to death. He knew what trouble their finances were in. He knew he hadn't sold a car in weeks. He knew that the commissions he was receiving wouldn't begin to support this new family. He knew his wife would have to quit work and not return for years. He would have to support the family fully and he was in trouble. He was worried, upset and bewildered. On Monday morning the sales manager again said, "I expect you to meet these goals." Bill walked out of the car showroom and stood on the front lot. He wanted to quit but he knew that he had to keep the job, keep it strong and keep the paychecks coming in. He had to sell cars. The expectation was set and he knew there were no choices.

Sometimes, our understanding of following Christ and leading others to be followers is filled with good feelings and happy thoughts. Yet, there is a reality of responsibility and duty even when it's not easy or fun. Bill's experience in car sales is a reminder of the practical experience that many people have when they are given opportunities to share Christ. Sometimes, we do it because we must, because it's our duty and responsibility, not because it is fun at the moment, we're in the mood or because it's easy. Too often, in considering hearing the faith, we are not honest with ourselves about our emotions and the difficulty of doing this task that Jesus asked.

Maybe we need to understand that Jesus said in His final instruction that we have no choice. We are to follow Him. We are told clearly that we must make disciples for Jesus Christ. Sometimes we take God's instructions so lightly. Making disciples is God's clear instruction. We do evangelism because we as disciples are instructed to. It may not be painless or pleasant, but it is right. It is easy for us to want every aspect of being a Christian to be deeply satisfying. The history of the Church is filled with stories of Christians doing the right thing because it was right and true, not because it was a bucket of laughs. There is a deep joy in sharing the story of Jesus. There is a great reward for those who decide to follow that story and live the Jesus way. But we need to remember, it's not always fun and easy.

Do Whatever Is Necessary

The problem with passion for evangelism is that often we don't realize what the goals are in being a Christian. In First Corinthians 9:19–27, Paul describes this by saying he would do all things that were necessary in order to reach new people for Christ. The key to successful sharing of the faith, leading other people to Christ and building the church is our passion, our commitment, our decision that this is a priority. As a young pastor I really had a hard time with this passage. I thought Paul was saying he would do anything to lead someone to Christ. Evangelism must be our passion by this clear definition in First Corinthians.

Certainly people have a variety of reasons for being evangelistic. Churches are in financial difficulty. They need new members. The pastor and lay leaders want to recruit new folks. Like a civic club that wants to influence the community by choosing influential people and great leaders to recruit for membership, pastors and lay leaders seek to influence the community, be more prestigious and feel better about themselves. So they recruit the wealthy, the powerful, the elite. Denominational executives set goals for local churches including membership increases, monetary goals and goals for the number of people who profess their faith. Pastors and church leaders who become fearful of repercussions of not making the goals, fearful of punishment or loss of their job become motivated to be evangelistic and invite new people to join the church. There are all kinds of reasons why people are evangelistic. Through institutional survival, vocational success or prestige the net results may be that people find the power of God's love in their life.

The Joy

The task of evangelism is one that takes passion, preparedness and purpose. It is not based on crisis, prestige or survival but upon commitment to Jesus. This is what Jesus asked us to do. We do this because we know the joy and the power of following Christ. We know that authentic healthy living comes out of this commitment. We do it because we know it is right and it is the thing that the Creator of the universe would want us to do. It is out of that sense of joy, satisfaction, justice and human purpose that we are committed and motivated to lead new people to Jesus Christ. We do this because we love God and we love what He has done for us.

The evangelism committee of the church had dismissed. Nathan and George were in the parking lot, talking about scores of local sports teams and then the conversation switched to the evangelism meeting. In the meeting they had been talking about getting members for the church. George made his opinions clear; he spoke with a sense of conviction. He said, "I heard all that discussion tonight in the meeting and I believe we've got to do something about our membership. It's evident we're all getting older; there are no young people in this church. We have a big debt on the church, and most of the members of our church are in retirement and have little money. If we're going to keep from going bankrupt, we've got to get some new, younger members with some money. All this talk about sharing Christ is important, but we need some results, or we're going bankrupt." His friend was stunned by the point-blank attitude of membership recruitment. Nathan understood the logic of membership recruitment; it was the simple fact that George was speaking about; the church needed more members, like a civic club or a business that needs more customers. The church could not make it without more members, healthy members, and yet Nathan knew that was not the right reason.

Many churches across America are caught in this dilemma of decline and it's easy to become panicked about it in terms of wanting to deal with the socioeconomic crisis that's created by a church or any organization with a continued decline in numbers of members or customers. Yet, that's not what Jesus asked us to deal with. Our evangelistic activities certainly do accomplish some of those goals of more people, more young people, more rich people, and yet that's not its purpose. Nathan, that night, simply couldn't be quiet. He said quietly to George, "I understand what you mean, George, and I know you're right about all of our needs." Nathan chose his words carefully, as he wanted George to understand why he believed in reaching new people and said it simply. "George, I've found that what Jesus Christ taught, is what we need to know and believe in, His principles of love and justice, of responsibility and integrity are imperatives. George, I believe that the Great Commandments really summarize the whole thing: we're to love God and love each other like we love ourselves. I know the people who don't have that love, who are self-centered and angry and depressed, and I don't want to be that way. Christianity is about God loving me, forgiving me and helping me. Jesus was about teaching me to believe in the worth of every person. It is really good news! People need Jesus! Following Christ is good." It is fantastic, satisfying, joyful, rewarding, comforting and empowering!

Questions for Discussion and Personal Reflection

1. Consider how evangelism is or is not like fishing.
2. Six steps in fishing are mentioned in the text. Evaluate how these steps are like leading someone to Christ.
3. Why are some Christians reluctant to evangelize?
4. Prayerfully consider First Corinthians 9:19–27 and what it means to you.
5. Outline your own personal plan to lead people to Christ.
6. Outline what the church needs to do to help.
7. Pray for joy in evangelism.

Chapter 5
Behaviorist Theology or Christyle

So often the motivation for evangelism is associated with guilt or fear. We must do it or we will be condemned, judged and found guilty. Too often the motivation and passion that is called for in biblical descriptions of evangelism are turned into self-righteous practices to prove that we are better than another Christian. The motivation for reaching new people may be financial. "We need the money for the church" or "We need more young people." But what is the real motivation?

The real motivation for being an evangelist is following Jesus. So many times, the practical motivations that might be better described as membership development become ineffective in keeping us on track in reaching new people for Christ. To do it just because we need more members who are wealthy or young may be good membership development strategy, but, over a long period of time, we need much more depth in our motivation to continue to share the Gospel of Jesus Christ with our friends, relatives, neighbors and acquaintances. As I have taught evangelism in so many different settings to so many different churches and denominational groups, I have found that, so often, the biggest problem is not understanding how but keeping the motivation clear and strong. It's being determined to share the faith even when the rewards aren't clear, the situation isn't easy and the mood isn't right. We share the Gospel because Jesus taught us to do that. The Great Commission in Matthew 28 says it without any question: we are called to be evangelists, to do what Jesus said.

How Great It Is

The five of them had created an accountability group. It was a group of church members who were part of the men's group in that county seat town church. They knew each other well, went to football games together and decided they needed to pray together, study the Bible together and hold each other in accountability about being Christians and members of the church. Tim brought it up as they finished breakfast that morning, "You know it is pretty evident our church needs some younger members. Last Sunday the pastor spoke about a new evangelism program, a kind of new membership drive. It seems to me that we ought to help, because we are all getting older and the church will die if we don't bring in some new younger members. I think we all ought to help with this program." Ed finished his coffee and got ready to leave. Before he left he said, "You know I agree. I'm on the finance committee and things haven't been good. With the death of three of our major contributors during the past two years we have really been hurt financially. We must have some new members that are contributing well. Sometimes I think we have to explain it clearly that joining the church is like joining anything else. You have to pay your dues. And we have a lot of people who aren't paying their dues. I think we need to recruit some new members, whether they are young or not I don't care. We need people who will give money to the church. We aren't going to make it unless we have more good givers." That started a discussion that went on for some time, making a couple of the members of the group late for work that morning. The discussion was about evangelism, membership recruitment, commitment and who they should invite and how they should invite them. Before the breakfast meeting ended, Darren had joined the group. He was the youngest one, the newest Christian and usually the most skeptical. Darren put it very bluntly, "I don't agree with you guys. If we are going to ask people to come to church it isn't because we want their money, although that is nice. It isn't because we want their age group for membership. The reason why we should invite people to come to church is because that is what Jesus told us to do. You guys have talked to me a lot about being a disciple. Isn't that what this is about? It is doing it because it's what Jesus would do. It is doing it because it's so great to be a Christian! I want to share it! I want to ask my friends to follow Jesus and find out how great it is. I want to share the faith because Jesus told me to. It is who I am, my identity."

The stories that are told in this chapter are stories about the practical activities of Christians of all groups and cultures. The common thread that runs through it all is it's a story of Christians finding a way to share the truth that they believe in and live by. Christianity is a faith that calls people to respect others. It's a faith that teaches us to love others. Being an evangelist must be out of the context of respect and love, but it also must be clear and done with integrity. The chapters that will follow are chapters that will seek to give instruction on how in our present culture we can share this good news. So many aspects of our culture would shove us into being quiet about our faith, would frighten us by the criticism of the culture and media of some Christian behavior. It may confuse us because of the multiplicity of understandings that make it so complicated to share the faith. But the experience that Christians have with God's love and truth make it worth it.

There are many great theologians that have guided the Church in the various circumstances in which the Church finds itself. Among those theologians, the name Charles Sheldon is not often found. Yet, this Kansas theologian, writing at the end of the nineteenth century, provided a theological understanding that is powerful and clear in terms of what it is to be a Christian. His theology is some of the most important for our understanding the Christian faith today.

In His Steps

In 1896 a Kansas pastor who was struggling with the meaning of commitment and what it meant to be a follower of Jesus wrote a novel. The story was simply about a congregation finding that they were not following the authentic power of the Gospel as they dealt with crisis in their local church. Out of that they made the decision that they were called to simply follow Jesus, what Jesus taught. The book was called *In His Steps*. It became a national best seller because it outlined living the Christian life in a practical day-to-day way.

Charles Sheldon influenced the history of Christian thought in a significant way by placing the emphasis upon behavior. So often, we place the emphasis on experience, belief or decision: Do you believe in Jesus? Have you experienced the power of Christ? Have you made a decision to commit your life? Those are all important aspects of our faith journey; yet, in the end, the question is whether or not we are doing it. The Sermon on the Mount ends with an interesting description. Jesus describes a house on a rock and a house on the sand. The winds come and the storms come, and the house on the rock stands, while the one built on the sand floats away. He then explains, *"The rain came down, the streams rose, and the winds blew and beat against that house; yet it did not fall, because it had its foundation on the rock. But everyone who hears these words of mine and does not put them into practice is like a foolish man who built his house on sand. The rain came down, the streams rose, and the winds blew and beat against that house, and it fell with a great crash"* (Matt. 7:25–27). The key is our behavior.

As we seek to claim the passion of evangelism the simple straightforward way of discussing it is to understand that this is what it means to follow Jesus. It is what Jesus asked us to do. The classical, theological description of the nature of Christ is that He is our Lord and Savior. Most often the theology of salvation is expressed by Christians in terms of the concept of the atonement:

Christ died for you. He shed His blood upon the cross for our redemption. Certainly gratitude is a way of expressing our commitment. Certainly we should give thanks that our sins are forgiven, that God loves us so much that He gave His Son. He gave us this gift, that if we believed in Him we would not perish but have eternal life. This becomes a beautiful way of discussing our commitment. Yet the other side of that simple definition of the nature of Christ is as powerful as the theology of the atonement and the realization that Christ is our Savior.

This theological concept affirms that Christ is our Lord, He is our leader. As Peter said, *"For to this you were called, because Christ suffered for you, leaving you an example, that you should follow in his steps"* (1 Peter 2:21). He is our King, He is our boss. In the world of business, military, government and family life, we search for leaders who will show us the way. Who do we trust? Who gives us the direction and the vision? Charles Sheldon in his book *In His Steps,* simply points out that Jesus is our Lord. He is the One who shows us how to live. Our passion as a Christian comes from that decision that Jesus is Lord. We belong to Him. He is our King, our Lord, our master, our director, our boss, our superintendent and our example. Jesus put it simply and clearly, "Go make disciples."

The local church seeks to encourage people to be personal witnesses, to share the faith and lead others to Christ. The motivations of success, financial problems, community prestige or vocational success may work for a moment, but they can pass quickly. The commitment to Jesus Christ as our Lord is basic and fundamental. Trying to encourage others to be witnesses by telling them that we need new members, to suggest that they will be rewarded in heaven or affirming that our particular local church is best only creates an unhealthy and temporary motivation. Too often we motivate and create evangelists for a short time, and then the motivation wears away.

The real motivation for evangelism must be total commitment, the belief that Jesus Christ is our Lord and Savior. All the descriptions of personal witnessing in the next chapters of this book are superficial and hollow if we are not committed to Jesus Christ as our Lord. Witnessing becomes some type of a gimmick if it is not based upon our passion to follow Christ no matter what.

When Paul says he will do what is necessary to become all things for all people in order to win someone for Christ, he lays out the priority. We are called to do the same. In First Corinthians 9:19–27 Paul makes some radical kinds of statements. He says,

> *Though I am free and belong to no one, I have made myself a slave to everyone, to win as many as possible. To the Jews I became like a Jew, to win the Jews. To those under the law I became like one under the law (though I myself am not under the law), so as to win those under the law. To those not having the law I became like one not having the law (though I am not free from God's law but am under Christ's law), so as to win those not having the law. To the weak I became weak, to win the weak. I have become all things to all people so that by all possible means I might save some. I do all this for the sake of the gospel, that I may share in its blessings. Do you not know that in a race all the runners run, but only one gets the prize? Run in such a way as to get the prize. Everyone who competes in the games goes into strict training. They do it to get a crown that will not last, but we do it to get a crown that will last forever. Therefore I do not run like someone running aimlessly; I do not fight like a boxer beating the air. No, I strike a blow to my body and make it my slave so that after I have preached to others, I myself will not be disqualified for the prize.*

It seems he says the end justifies the means. Most Christians have trouble with the philosophy, yet Paul is trying to explain that he will do what is necessary to lead someone to Christ. Paul's willingness to take it that far is a way of explaining to us how important it is to share the Gospel. It is not something to do it if you have time, if it is convenient. It is a priority!

In a sense, Paul says he will try to relate to the individual he is witnessing to. He is saying that results are what matters. In these passages he is placing himself, his own vulnerability and even his integrity far below the importance of telling the world about Jesus Christ. It may seem hard for us to accept the practical ethics of what Paul is teaching in this theological statement, yet the emphasis should be easy to understand. Sometimes, we are not willing to do difficult, complicated actions in order to bring the results that the Bible teaches. Yet, we are called to be faithful, even when it is difficult.

Our faith is shown by our behavior. James tells us in James 2:26 that he wanted us to be clear about the importance of doing the faith. He simply said that faith without works or action does not exist. In these teachings James makes it clear that being a follower of Jesus Christ takes more than talk, more than belief, it takes action. It is the imperative to do what Jesus taught. Charles Sheldon's book *In His Steps* models that struggle from over a hundred years ago. The book captures the struggle that every Christian has. We like being a Christian, we love the power of God's Spirit and the comfort of His love, yet so often we spend our time saying, "Lord, Lord" rather than really doing what Jesus told us to do.

At the end of Matthew's gospel and in the first part of the story of the early church in the book of Acts we are presented with the last words of Jesus, His instructions. We were told to go and make disciples. In Matthew 25, Jesus describes three kinds of behavior. All are evaluated as good or bad. We are told to be ready and if we are not ready we will be shut out. We are told in that same chapter to do our best with our talents and if we don't they will be taken away. The chapter ends where Jesus tells us clearly that, unless we help our neighbors in their times of need, we will not enter the kingdom of heaven. Every one of these examples is an example of behavior. We are saved by our faith in Jesus Christ. But as James makes it clear, *"faith by itself, if it has no works, is dead"* (James 2:17).

The Christyle

The novel *In His Steps* written by Charles Sheldon tells the story of a group of Christians who decided their faith was based upon doing what Jesus would do. First Peter 2:21 contains the instructions that God sent Christ to be an example to follow in His steps. The idea of following in the steps of Jesus is explained clearly in Christ's own teaching, particularly in the synoptic gospels. Paul, Peter, James and John each wrote about doing the faith. James provides a fantastic argument throughout his writings to help us understand that faith is what we do. It is through our behavior that we show our faith. Charles Sheldon is not known as a great theologian of the church and yet he presented a practical, common sense understanding of being a Christian that is behavioralistic. It is accountable. It is what Jesus clearly speaks of in Matthew 25 when He describes Christianity in terms of behavior. He ends the Sermon on the Mount by saying not everyone who says "Lord, Lord" shall enter the kingdom, but those who do the will of my heavenly father (Matt. 7:21). Note the emphasis is on behavior, on action. He says those who do my will are like a house built on a rock. Again the standard for being a Christian is our behavior. When a person seeks what it is to be a follower of Jesus, the answer is simply to do what He would do.

The word "Christyle" is a word I created by combining the words "Christ" and "style," for that simply is what it is to be a Christian. It is to combine our doing with our being. So joining the two words together is a simple way to speak about being a Christian. Charles Sheldon provided a simple way for ordinary people to understand what it is to be a Christian: Follow in His steps. The reason we share our faith or witness or tell others the story of Christ is because that is what we are asked to do by Jesus Christ. It is making our behavior fit our belief. It is combining our doing with our being. It is the Christyle.

I have often called this behavioristic belief; that is, Christian behavior that fits our beliefs. Christians affirm all kinds of beliefs and, yet, one of the greatest criticisms of Christians today is that we're hypocritical. We say one thing and do another. The Christyle is a theological approach that emphasizes our behavior as well as our beliefs. It is doing what Jesus taught.

So often, one criticism of Christianity is that we say one thing and then do another. In this so-called Post-Christian Age, Christians are oftentimes criticized for their hypocrisy. Jesus emphasized it over and over and over—it is our behavior that shows our faith. Evangelism then becomes a way of showing our faith, our commitment. To put it in the opposite way, the motivation for doing evangelism is not just to get new members or deal with the financial problems in the church; our reason is that it's what Jesus taught us to do.

The Goal Is Leading People to Christ

It was a meeting of our church's administrative board, a critical meeting. The decision was whether or not we would add another worship service with a different style of music. The church had been in an uproar. There were members of the church that didn't want guitars and drums in worship. The contemporary worship team had practiced and there had been trial worship services where the congregation had been invited to participate. Some loved it and some did not. This was the board meeting to decide: Would we add a contemporary worship to the two traditional services? The discussion was hot and heavy. Most Christians have gone through a similar discussion about liturgy, music or some other aspect of worship. Most churches today struggle with starting new worship services as a way of reaching new people.

This was a tough meeting. Stan was a real estate salesman. He liked to stand in the front hallway and greet everyone with a big smile. Children, youth and old people loved Stan, and he loved the great traditions of the church. He had been a member of another church in town where they had a big fight and the church had broken apart because of some innovations in worship. He didn't want that to happen again. He didn't like contemporary music and he didn't want a contemporary service. He didn't like the idea of modern musical instruments being on the chancel. So when he stood to speak most people knew where he stood, or they thought they knew. Stan began by reviewing what had happened at the practice sessions. "I have been to those trial worship services, I have listened to the guitars and drums." Then he clearly stated, "I don't like the music, I don't like the drums, and I'm never going to attend another contemporary worship service at our church." Then he paused for a moment and said, "But I am going to vote for starting this new worship service tonight because I believe it will reach new people for Jesus Christ." He said, "We must do what Jesus taught. The goal is not having music that I like; it is leading people to Jesus." He made it clear that he was going to do what Jesus taught, and he did. Then with a twinkle in his eye he said, "I am going to vote for adding a new worship choice, and I will fight anyone of you who will vote against it." Everybody laughed and the vote was taken. Hundreds of people were led to Christ over the next five years because of that service. All Paul said was I will do what is necessary. That is what Stan did, and that is what we must do.

This book is filled with many ideas and suggestions for how to reach people for Christ. Stan's decision to vote for the contemporary worship service in the story above provides the simple guidelines for how we make decisions about programs, activities and ministries that may or may not be evangelistic. The question is: Will it reach new people for Christ? Will it do what Jesus taught us to do? Jesus did not teach us that a particular kind of music, vocabulary or particular way of articulating the Christian faith is correct. He did teach us that we are to make disciples; that is correct. Therefore, our decisions follow what Christ taught.

On this particular evening of the evangelism committee meeting, we had an extra large crowd; some extra people had come to the meeting. The church had worked hard on following the Christyle, making decisions based upon what Jesus would do, understanding that's the basis of evangelism. So we learned soon into the meeting that it was not just an ordinary church committee meeting. We were going to deal with the issue in an unusual way but it was clear, the question was, "What would Jesus do?" Three guys were present at the meeting, all bringing a proposal. "Let's have a car show on the front parking lot," a simple idea. Bring in lots of rebuilt, unusual cars; lots of people would come by the church, stop in, see where the church is; it would attract some attention and be an invitational event. Others on the committee asked, "Isn't this a little manipulative? We try to get a crowd by waving a car show flag and not really sharing Christ?" The three guys had their answers put together well; they had heard the Christyle and understood about what Jesus would do. They explained that their buddies who came to car shows and exhibited at car shows were mostly non-Christian. This would give them a chance to be at church, a chance for us to share the faith, a chance for us to witness. How would you have decided that evening in the car show discussion at the evangelism committee meeting? It's also easy to decide what Jesus would really do. But when we are making decisions in terms of spreading the Gospel of Jesus Christ, we need to ask ourselves what is effective, appropriate and true. Those are hard questions about what the best thing to do and the most effective way to lead people to Christ. I am continually haunted by the words of Paul that I've mentioned several times in this book. He said simply in First Corinthians 9:22 (WEB), *"I have become all things to all men, that I might by all means save some."*

The focus of this chapter has been upon behavior, understanding that to be a Christian, it is not just what we say or commit to; it's what we do. This understanding, which I have called behavioristic Christianity, makes it clear that sharing the faith is what we do. We are called to be evangelists not only by what we say but by how we share the love of Jesus Christ in our lives.

Questions for Discussion and Personal Reflection

1. Take a moment and consider how guilt and fear has been used to motivate us to become more evangelistic or to share the faith. Then consider the effect of that kind of negative motivation.
2. Consider the idea of following in the steps of Jesus as proclaimed by Charles Sheldon. What would it mean to be motivated to share the faith in a positive way?
3. If you had been with the followers of Jesus when He spoke to them as recorded in Matthew 28–The Great Commission–how would you have responded?
4. List your understanding of the goals of the church, and consider how evangelism or leading people to Christ is a major goal.

Chapter 6
Tell

In the process of remembering and following important sets of ideas, human beings naturally try to label them to create a way of remembering and an approach to teaching. We have chosen to use the word "TELL."

Andrew rushed to "tell" his brother Simon Peter about Jesus (John 1:41). Jesus described the task of a Christian in the ascension statement in Matthew 28:16–20 in terms of "telling." The early followers of Jesus on the day of Pentecost went into the streets to "tell" the people of Jerusalem about Jesus (Acts 2). The world of the 21st century is a world of communications. The use of the Internet and all forms of electronic communication devices amplifies our desire to "tell" others. Through technology the world is becoming a "Global Village." Sales and business success is built upon the concept that satisfied customers and clients will "tell" their friends.

Human beings have always been storytellers, information tellers, truth tellers, even non-truth tellers. We have been exact and we have exaggerated. We have been truthful and we have been liars. We have told stories that have created wars, and stories that have created great acts of generosity. It is through our communications that the finest and worst examples of human behavior are seen. Some have described this immediate access to communication as flattening our world, meaning we all have access to the same amount of information and the same instruments of telling. However we want to describe it, we need to understand we have become linked together as family, friends and community. The world has become a village. It is in this village we are asked to tell the story of Jesus. The task of evangelism involves telling. To TELL is our task!

This Book Is Divided

In a sense, this book is divided into two parts. One deals with telling or sharing the faith as an individual, the second deals with sharing the faith as a church. These two parts must go together. We do not share the faith alone, we do it within the community of followers of Jesus Christ that we call the church. At the same time the church can do much but it must finally be the individual who takes responsibility to tell the story and to do the task. Therefore, the following summary of the concept of TELL is an introduction that will be described in detail in the following chapters. We will first describe TELL as an individual process then as a group process. Evangelism is not a task to be done alone; rather it is the task of the individual as a part of the church.

Truth

The four letters in the word "TELL" can provide for us an instruction in how to "go fish."

The witness of an individual Christian and the church is the witness of telling the story. The letters in the English word TELL remind us of some essential aspects of our telling the story. The T reminds us of truth. The most powerful way in which we can convey the power and integrity of the Gospel is the truth of our own lives. It is to be able to tell our story. It is how the power of God's Holy Spirit has changed our life. The truth is how the message of Jesus has given us answers for the basic questions of our life. We are told by Jesus "You will know the truth, and the truth will make you free" (John 8:32 NAS). This truth is essential for making decisions today. We have so many alternatives, so many choices and yet in the truth of Jesus Christ we have answers that work. To use the word truth as a way of reminding us how we witness is to remind us that the integrity of what we say is a critical issue. Secular, non-Christian people probably can understand Jesus Christ best from our own personal story, the truth of what we have experienced.

Some might describe the importance of the truth in discussing belief. Belief is understood in many different ways. Some who study human behavior suggest belief is the key to behavior. Our beliefs influence our attitudes and values, and our attitudes and values set our behavior. If we believe that people of a different race, gender or ethnicity are inferior we will behave that way towards them. If we believe in loving our neighbor, we act in a loving way. If we believe in a God who created us, that belief will dictate our behavior, our discussions and our values. Therefore the truth about our life, what we have experienced, who we are and what we believe is essential in sharing the faith. It is the key. If we try to share the faith without believing, a secular society will see through our hypocrisy. Our best way of sharing our beliefs is through the truth of our own lives.

Explaining

The E in the word TELL reminds us of the word explain. In other generations when we describe the task of telling the world of the Gospel of Jesus Christ, the word "explain" was simply an assumption that no one thought a whole lot about. Explaining was common in a culture that was strongly Christian. Explaining was not always necessary, most people had heard the details of Christ's life, the story of His birth, life and resurrection. They knew about the church. They probably attended church. Their friends and family had already informed them about the beliefs of a Christian. That culture has radically changed today. People don't understand what Christianity is about. Many times secular, non-Christian people do not understand it. They may have received an explanation from the common media that is not the truth.

We need to be explainers. It means we must be systematic theologians, able not only to explain but to explain in a way that makes sense, in a way that relates to the other truths. Explaining opens the door to our story and our invitations, but often, unless we explain well, we never get the opportunity to really touch someone's life. The skeptical attitudes toward Christians, the criticism of Christian hypocrisy, the sarcastic criticism of evangelical Christians by our culture means that Christians must know what they believe and how to explain it. Explain it in a way that makes sense not just for the Christian but for the most secular individual. Explaining is a major task and it opens the door for telling the story of Jesus Christ.

Explaining is basic to our nature. Everybody wants to know what is going on: Would you explain what the problem is, would you explain what the government is doing, would you explain what the boss said, would you explain what you meant? Explaining is that continual task of helping people know the meaning, purpose and direction.

In the non-Christian world in which we are called to witness, the culture continually reports on issues of religion and spirituality, often incorrectly or with a bias or even with intentional misinformation. Our job as Christians is to explain, and our explaining gives us an opportunity to tell the truth. A friend might ask why churches have such different kinds of music. The explanation can be an opportunity to talk about the importance of worship, what the purpose and meaning of worship is and how different kinds of music can support different kinds of worship. At the same time, it gives the opportunity to explain the truth about why we worship and the deep satisfaction that comes to all of us as we worship. In this highly secular world where people speak about disinterest in church and religion, but great interest in spirituality, we are provided an open door to explain. And in explaining we can share the truth of Jesus Christ.

Live

To tell the truth and to explain are done most often by simply speaking, writing or emailing. Yet one of the most effective ways of witnessing is not by the words we use but by the identity of who we are. The first L in TELL reminds us of a simple principle that is critically important: We must live the faith. Our culture is filled with a seemingly endless hunger for detailed information about everyone. Whether it is a politician or your own parents we want to know who they really are. We want to see and experience the values, beliefs and ideas in their life. To live the Christian faith is one of the clearest ways of sharing the Gospel of Jesus Christ in this skeptical world. The post-modern media have chosen to characterize the Christian in terms of our sins and we are often described as hypocrites. Hypocrisy seems to be one of the greatest turn offs in our world today. We want people to be authentic, not fake, "warts and all." So we must share the Gospel of Jesus Christ authentically in the way we live.

Living opens doors. The young woman says to her coworker in a busy office, "I just watch you and I'm amazed. You seem to handle things with a different attitude than so many of us have. You are so compassionate and so caring. What is it about you?" And the door of communication is open to tell the truth and to explain. In the word TELL the L isn't the first letter, but it might be the most important one. Unless we live the faith, unless we are authentic, whatever we say sounds like hypocrisy.

One of the clearest ways we can live the faith is by doing what Jesus continually coached us to do, to help. Matthew 25 says that what we do for others, how we help others is the key to our eternal life. Jesus went about helping and caring. One of the clearest ways we witness to the Gospel of Jesus Christ is by being people who care. The church's authentic living must be one of caring and meeting needs. The church is accused of being irrelevant, yet when the church offers cancer support groups or when the pastor is willing to stay late to help a marriage that is having great difficulties, then the church is there to help and meet real needs. There is an authenticity to living the faith when we live it by helping. The Good Samaritan model should be the model for all of us. Jesus concluded his story of the Good Samaritan by saying, *"Go and do likewise"* (Luke 10:37). We are to be Good Samaritans by helping people with real needs. It is by our compassion, care, patience and determination that we show Jesus Christ.

Living a Christian life may be the simplest part of witnessing, yet often it is the hardest part. We can tell a story of our own encounter with the power of Christ in our lives, we can explain about Jesus, but when it comes to living the Gospel, our sinful natures get in the way. God doesn't expect us to be perfect. Even secular people who are hearing our witnessing realize that all of us have faults and make mistakes. Paul says in the Bible that *"all have sinned and fall short of the glory of God"* (Rom. 3:23). Yet even with our imperfections we must show the results of the experience of Jesus Christ in our personal lives. Living becomes the bottom line. The skeptical critic of Christianity, the lonely secular person, the lost soul searching for the way all need to know the Gospel of Jesus Christ. They need to see it in our lives, our attitudes, our positive spirit, our hopeful purpose and our practical living skills.

Mom had prepared a beautiful birthday cake. The icing flowed over the cake into the edge of the plate. The birthday party was later that day. The cake sitting on the kitchen counter was a great temptation. Jimmy stood with his eyes even with the top of the cabinet, directly across from his eyes and nose was that beautiful icing, and all it would take was a quick finger and no one would ever know. He paused with his finger ready to take a dip while his mom was away, then he turned around to look over his right shoulder when he heard the small voice of his little sister. She was somewhere behind him and she was asking him a question. With his finger ready to swipe into the icing he heard her cry. He remembered what his dad said the night before, that he was to be a leader for his little sister. He was the big brother, and his dad was proud of him for the good things he was doing to help his sister. As easy as it would be to dip into the icing, and as much as he wanted it, he realized she was watching. He didn't want her to see him. He realized he had a responsibility for his behavior. We must realize that we live in a very permissive society that promotes dipping into the icing whenever we please. We live in a world that seems to operate with no morality or integrity at all. We must ask ourselves about our responsibility for being an example to others. It is not just "will we get caught," it's "will we do the right thing?" The first L is for living the faith.

Lead

The last L in TELL is a reminder of our responsibility to be leaders. It would be so easy to tell our story, explain our beliefs, live a Christian life and yet never lead others to Christ. One of the strongest aspects of our witnessing for the faith is to lead. Leading can be done in many ways. Often it is simply inviting, "Would you come to church with me?" "Would you join me in a Bible study?" "Would you have time for us to talk?" "Would you help me take dinner to the homeless shelter?" "Would you help me organize a support group for grandparents raising their grandchildren?" To lead is to be willing to go the second mile, to be willing to take a stand, to really care and to invite.

Leading involves inviting someone to accept Jesus Christ as their Lord and Savior, not out of arrogance but rather out of a genuine desire to help them. The invitation is Christian leadership. It is not demanding or pushy; it is genuine, loving and powerful.

To lead a person to follow Christ is the most important part of telling the story. It is inviting someone to make the decision that will transform their life and empower their future. Our goal is to lead people to become fully devoted followers of Jesus Christ. The following chapters will first outline how we share the faith as individuals, and then how we share the faith as a church.

Questions for Discussion and Personal Reflection

1. Spend a few moments reviewing in your mind the various ways the church over the years has encouraged us to share our faith or tell others about Jesus Christ.
2. Remember in your own life a time when you heard someone describing evangelism, sharing or witnessing, and how that was explained.
3. Contrast the circumstances in our culture today with the circumstances in the past as faith was shared.
4. How can the four letters in the word TELL, which remind us of Truth, Explain, Live and Lead, help us to share the Gospel?
5. How can you communicate the truth of your own spiritual journey and your own conviction to people around you, family and friends?
6. Make a list of the things that you would need to explain to a person today who didn't know Jesus.
7. Describe why living the faith is so important in sharing the faith.
8. How do we lead people to Christ today? List examples.

Chapter 7
Truth

The infomercial comes across the TV screen, the salesperson demonstrates the product with much enthusiasm and we wonder *is it really true?* The used car salesman shouts in a loud voice that echoes around the living room of your home, telling you that he has "such a deal!" In the midst of all the noise we wonder if it really is a good deal. We want to know the truth. Does it work? Will it last? Can I use it? Will it help my life?

Reality World

We are in a "reality TV" world. Television program after program focuses upon reality, how people really feel and deal with unusual living conditions, challenges and opportunities. We love to watch the real-life stories of families with lots of children or lots of problems. In a TV series someone is chosen whom the audience now knows "too much" about. Life is depicted with all of its reality. We love to watch and call it entertainment. We have become people who want to know what is real, what is true, what works and what doesn't work. Whether it's a candidate for political office or our friend in the next cubicle, we want to know the truth about their lives, what they think and how they feel. There was a time when this compulsion for the truth seemed obnoxious, unnecessary and inappropriate. There are personality types that just don't like to "let it all hang out." They are private, controlled. Yet it now seems necessary to have a sense of authenticity about who we are and what we believe in order to communicate realistically in this culture.

I sat in a seminary class on preaching and the professor said, "Never use a personal illustration in your sermon. Take it from a book, a play, a public figure. People don't want to know your personal life." I thought that professor was right. Today if the pastor never shares their personal feelings in the sermon, he or she is seen as inauthentic, distant and uncaring.

These examples are simply reminders of a cultural shift to openness and transparency. But for the Christian who wants to share the Gospel of Jesus Christ it opens a fantastic opportunity. We can share what Jesus means to us, how His teachings help us, what it means to feel the love of God. Your story is the first line of witnessing to anyone else. It is not effective to seem arrogant or self-righteous. The "I have found Jesus, what's wrong with you?" style of evangelism does not work. We must be honest and simply share, "I have found in God's love through the teachings and experience of Christ, a change that really works for me." The stories of our journey in life and how our faith has made the difference are stories that empower others. Worship services that are effective today are often punctuated by personal testimonies because that's what we want to know.

Arrogant Evangelism

In the Christian culture of the contemporary church some might say evangelism has become a dirty word. We don't want to talk about evangelism, leading people to Christ, witnessing or sharing the faith. Some don't want to talk about growth. It all sounds too commercial, too egotistical. In most churches, if the pastor was to announce that next Sunday his sermon topic would be how to be a witness, attendance might be down significantly. The problem is that witnessing or sharing the faith has a bad reputation.

Some Christians have shared their faith in such an egotistical, arrogant way that many have concluded they don't want to do evangelism. There was a time the motivation for being an evangelist was "We have found the way and you don't know where you are going!"

I remember earlier in my ministry the community where I served as pastor brought in a nationally known evangelist. He suggested the theme for his evangelistic crusade was "I found it." We all wore badges that stated "I found it!" To the non-Christian it was the Christians saying "I found it, what is wrong with you?" and, "I have found something good and you don't have it." It was a way of saying "I'm better than you."

As Christians we feel that being a follower of Jesus, receiving the joy of God's love through Christ and the power of the Holy Spirit are things that are extremely wonderful. And they are. Yet it shouldn't create in us an attitude of arrogance. To be a follower of Christ is to become a person of love. Paul says clearly all the law and all the commandments can be summarized very simply as loving your neighbor as yourself. Paul describes, *"Love is patient, love is kind. It does not envy, it does not boast, it is not proud. It does not dishonor others, it is not self-seeking, it is not easily angered, it keeps no record of wrongs. Love does not delight in evil but rejoices with the truth"* (1 Cor. 13:4–6). That description should be the basis for the way we witness. We shouldn't witness in an arrogant, self-righteous, egotistical way. We shouldn't share the faith in a way that puts others down or makes them feel ridiculed. We shouldn't share the faith in a way that calls non-Christians names. In today's highly secular, post-modern era those techniques do not work.

Antidote for Hypocrisy

We are at a time where Christians are being criticized regularly in the media for hypocrisy. We are at a time where evangelistic Christians are seen as the enemies of common sense, of collegiality, goodwill and friendship. Part of the reason for this is because of the arrogant way in which we sought to share the faith. John said, "Whoever does not love does not know God, for God is love" (1 John 4:8). Therefore our sharing of the faith must be done in the context of love. The old arrogant self-righteous way is simply not the way that Christ taught. People receiving our witness, who listen to our story, who respond to our invitation must do it because we are sharing Christ even in the way we do it. The love of Jesus Christ must be seen in our language, in our demeanor and in the body posture of our relationships. People are not brought to the awareness of the loving power of Jesus Christ by arrogant, self-righteous, judgmental people who put down their friends and try to scare them into heaven.

Two weeks after their grandmother had died, two sisters sat at the table having breakfast with their father. They began to talk about their grandmother, and then the girls changed the focus and asked their father what he believed about eternal life and where Grandmother was. He had always gone to church and he had taken the girls to church, yet he was of the old school of "don't really reveal to anyone what you are and what you believe." Yet there they were asking all of those questions—private questions, personal questions, and he had to answer. They had struggled in their family. The girls had drifted away from church and one of them was angry about some things that had happened. He was disappointed in them because he felt they had never really given the way of Jesus a try. They had always been skeptical and his loyalty to the church didn't seem apparent at all to them. They thought it was some kind of routine ritual, a superfluous activity. Both girls were in their 20s and hadn't been to church in years. That morning at the breakfast table they were talking about God and faith and he simply broke through his barriers of reserve and told the girls about his own journey of faith, things he should have said to them long ago yet he had never really been able to. Now with his mother's death in front of him it seemed easier. He told them what Jesus meant to him. He described his own skepticism at their age and what he had been through. He described the struggles that he and their mother had with some of the things in their church, and how they had worked through those struggles. He told the girls how his faith in God had made such a difference in the way that he parented, the way he did his job, the way that he showed love. In that moment at the breakfast table his daughters finally understood. Like a magic door swung open by his words, they believed. They needed to know what the truth was, what their father believed in, yet he had never been able to tell them until that moment. Their lives were changed because of his truth and honesty.

Candid, Honest, Practical and Appropriate

Being candid, honest, practical and appropriate should to be the primary methodology in sharing our faith. Not every circumstance will offer an opportunity to be candid. Not every friend wants to know about your tough times in life or your acceptance of Christ. But we live in a culture that validates human experience by the truth that is lived out by practicing Christians. The barriers that have been put up by our secular society are simply melted away by honest sharing of what Jesus Christ means to you, honest sharing of how the theology of Christians explains life and directs our behavior. Charles Sheldon's simple idea of "What would Jesus do?" can become the theological way of authentically explaining what we have come to understand as our values and beliefs about what to do in life. Your story, if told in the context of seeking to follow Christ, can become amazingly simple to the skeptical, unsure friend.

We need to find the words that describe the truth about Christ in our personal lives. We need to find the theological words, made simple and secular, that explain the nature of Christ, the power of the Holy Spirit and the love of God. Sometimes we need to practice telling what we believe in and who we are. These beliefs generate the power of our own personal lives.

Summary

Often the truth of our own lives is complicated by difficulties, confusion and personal struggle. To be absolutely clear about our faith and to be able to articulate it without any questions can be extremely difficult. The essential thing is that we share the truth honestly and do not try to put up a pretense of perfection or over-simplification and instead say simply and honestly what Christ means to us.

A good summary of what it means to be a Christian could include a summary of knowing that we are loved by God, what some theologians call "grace." We all need self-esteem–knowing unequivocally that God loves us and resting in that security–is something the world chases after constantly. This is one of the essentials of our faith–knowing that we are forgiven and loved and that Jesus came to show us this in the most amazing way. The second point is that we have a purpose, that God loves us and that we are called to take up our cross daily and follow Him. Taking up our cross is not some terrible burden but a joy. Many recent publications have pointed out clearly that a sense of purpose and meaning is desperately needed for human beings, and that one of the greatest gifts of the Christian faith is its calling, meaning and purpose.

Finally, the Christian has a sense of right and wrong and a set of principles by which to live. Christ shows us how we should treat others and ourselves. These laws are clear and simple. In Luke 10, Jesus says that we are to love God with our heart, mind, soul and body, and to love our neighbors as ourselves. These principles guide us through life. The gift of being a Christian is that we have a sense of truth, and this is much to celebrate.

Guidelines

For many the question of how to share our story becomes a significant issue. Some of us talk too much and some of us talk too little. Some of us wander in our thinking and sharing and never get to the point. If we are at that moment where we can share the faith by sharing our story, we need to be ready. This means we need to practice. We need to think about it, we need to be sensitive and responsive. The following are some guidelines for sharing the faith.

1. Listen

First, listen. Unless we have taken the time to listen to our friend we will be off target in sharing. When you listen with an open mind you are not listening for a moment when your friend pauses and you can jam your particular story into the conversation. We need to listen so we understand our friend, where they hurt, what is going on, what their questions are, what their struggles are and what is their life journey. To be appropriate in our sharing we need to know who we are sharing with, how they hurt and what they think.

The first step is to listen and to listen carefully. In many ways most Christians need to take a class in listener training. We are enthusiastic about the Gospel, we love Jesus and our church is a main part of our lives, so why wouldn't we want to tell about it? Yet without listening we will probably not be heard. Our listening is to help us to understand the person we are sharing with, to help us understand their needs and interests, help us understand where they are open and where they are not.

As we listen we should ask ourselves: What is my friend interested in? What are the struggles my friend has experienced? Where have they been hurt? What were the bad experiences they had with other Christians and churches? How can my experiences be helpful and not arrogant? This beginning list of questions can help us form what we are going to share. Some groups suggest we practice how to listen and then how to share the faith.

2. Prepare

The second step after listening is to prepare. This does not mean we have a canned talk, a packaged presentation. It simply means we know the basics of our faith. We need to put together some words that make sense and can be helpful. We need to prepare; we need to practice doing this. The problem with practicing is when we think we have our story just right and all we need is an opening in the conversation to dump it in. When we approach it that way we are forcing our story on the other person. It should be that the other person will find our story helpful, interesting and that they will come to understand Jesus. We need to practice with that in mind.

We need to have spent some time in careful analysis of our own story. One of the first questions in examining our story is who is the hero in the story? If we are the hero, if the story is really about our magnificent accomplishments or our championing over difficulty, it is not necessarily going to lead someone to Christ. At best it may impress a friend concerning your abilities and at worst it will completely turn your friend off from learning more about Jesus. Stories can be about you, but the hero should always be Jesus Christ! They should tell what Christ has done in our lives. It is Christ we want to convey, not how clever, imaginative, tenacious or successful we are.

3. Relevancy

In doing the analysis of our story we need to think about what parts of our story will relate to the needs or situations of another person. If we have been through a divorce and our story of Christ's power in our life involves that divorce it is a relevant thing to share with another person going through a divorce. It may not be helpful to a friend who is angry because his daughter has just gone through divorce. The moment of extreme conviction that came to you at the point when you lost your job and were on the verge of financial disaster may be very relevant to many people, yet for some it may be the last thing that they need to hear about at that particular time. Our readiness, our analysis is effective in the context of listening and knowing about our friend that we are sharing with.

4. Appropriate

Another characteristic of our sharing is to be timely and appropriate. We need to know when to quit telling the story. I understand that the witnessing program of the Upper Room suggests a few minutes is long enough. That is probably good advice. We need to talk and share enough but not too much. Most of us are so enthusiastic about what Christ has done for our lives that we could share all evening. We could tell stories and give examples that have been important in our own lives. We could go on and on, however we should keep in mind that the most powerful commercials today are less than 60 seconds long. Most of the time we don't have to tell everything, just the points that are relevant and most helpful to that person.

5. Closing

We need to know how to close the story, whether the story ends with an invitation or not. If you are in a new relationship with a friend who is searching for faith, telling the story too soon may end with a full blown enthusiastic invitation to come to church or accept Christ that will probably be ineffective. As the saying goes, we need to "let go and let God." We need to be ready for questions. After we share out of our heart we need to be open to questions. We need to be ready for misunderstandings, for anger, for frustrations, for bewilderment, for silence. This is a part of the challenge. You don't know and you can't prepare except to be in prayer.

6. Trust

The final step is to trust in God for your witness to be effective, because God's Spirit is able to penetrate and change. One of the most difficult parts of sharing our faith is that we want to get it done, get it over with, make the sale, win the soul, recruit, save, change, rescue. This will happen through the power of the Holy Spirit and it may not happen at the time of our witness and sharing. It may be hours, weeks or years later.

Instruction for Telling Your Story

The following are the steps for telling your faith story. You may do these steps as a group–prayer group, Bible study group, group of friends interested in sharing or you may do it alone as individual prayer. It is an outline for how you might practice in telling the story. One of the things that is important is that your story does not need to be long. Practice telling your story in 100 words. It should be something that can be shared in less than five minutes with questions that might follow. Find a group where you can practice this, a group of committed Christians who understand what you're doing. This may be a regular exercise of your Bible study group, your prayer group or a group that's been formed to study this matter of how to share your faith. It's important that we become comfortable and natural in sharing and can share in a way that is authentic with our own journey.

The following are some steps to practice sharing your faith:

1. Begin with a time of prayer, asking God to reveal to you how to share your story of Christ's power with others.

2. Think of people you know or are associated with that would be helped by your story of God's power through Christ.

3. Spend some time describing these people, thinking about them, praying for them. List their characteristics, hurts and desires. In the next few weeks, spend time listening to them. Ask them questions. Interview them. Listen. Don't critique, just listen and affirm. Respond to their sharing with a simple question or "I understand" or just an affirmation of yes or okay.

4. Practice sharing your faith alone or with the trusted group.

5. An outline or notes for sharing your story:

   a. Understanding who you are sharing with–their hurts, desires, frustrations and phobias.

   b. Your story needs to be genuine and out of your own experience. It should relate to the experience of those with whom you are speaking.

   c. Your story needs to focus on God's power through Christ, not your heroic actions. Not your success, but how God helps you.

   d. Your story needs to end with a simple affirmation of God's power.

   e. Your story needs to be open to any questions that the person might have.

f. As you enter into telling the story, remember to be open to the need to change or adapt the story and respond to the guidance of the Holy Spirit.

g. After you have formulated your story, spend some time practicing it. Share it with a very trusted friend, or simply share it with God in a room by yourself in prayer. It is often helpful to tell your story out loud to God. Practice it, trying to keep it under 100 words.

h. Ask for God's guidance.

i. Finally, wait for the opportunity to tell your story.

Learning how to witness is a crucial step. Though the actual act of sharing our faith may not come in any formalized way with a five-minute presentation, it most likely will come as a part of the next steps, answering questions, living the faith, inviting. We need to be familiar with what our story is, what we believe, how we know God has affected us, what it means to be a follower of Jesus.

We need to be comfortable, flexible and articulate in showing. The coaching alone will help us be confident in our response. The story needs to be told out of the joy of being a Christian. So often in the past, stories of God's gift have emphasized more the negative of how bad we were or how bad the situation was. Certainly, that contrast of before and after is important, and yet, too many times, we have almost emphasized the tragedy of our experience in life so much that one might think we had to be terribly bad to ever be very good.

I remember a group of leaders in my second church asked that we start holding Wednesday night testimony meetings, and we did. The same leaders came back after six months and asked not to hold Wednesday night testimony meetings anymore because their testimonies were not near as good as some of the ornery members of the church and they were being embarrassed because they didn't have a story of their terrible misdeeds to make the story of their conversion to Christ better. Certainly, the negative parts of our story are important, but they are only an integrated part of the whole.

In this chapter, we have mentioned prayer often. Prayer is the key to making the truth clear for us in forming our story, in understanding who we are, in celebrating our journey. We need to be in prayer and ask for God's guidance and encouragement.

Questions for Discussion and Personal Reflection

1. Consider several situations when someone shared their honest, personal story with you. How did you feel? How did you react?
2. To help us to be loving and Christ-like in sharing our faith story, list the characteristics of loving and sharing.
3. Explain how we can listen in order to really understand who we are sharing with.
4. What are some examples of where you have shared your faith in an effective way with others?
5. Turn to the Appendix #1 and find a way to create a "Truth Sharing Group."
6. Talk to God and your friends about your story of God's truth in your life.

Chapter 8
Explain

Sean was going through that time in life that seems to happen just before adolescence, when we want to know "why" about everything. He was spending the night at his best friend's house, and when he was told that his friend's family was going to church the next morning Sean was filled with questions about what he was about to experience. What is church? Who is God? Why do they sing that music? On and on the questions came pouring out of his mind and mouth. He was ready to ask the questions and receive the answers. In that moment the young boy was ready to start learning about faith.

Explain Well

Our ability to explain to a 10-, 20- or 70-year-old is crucial in our witnessing. The confusing illustrations of faith given by so much of the media, the public criticisms of hypocrisy and the sometimes silly things that Christians do in the name of faith all generate questions. Why are they taking that offering? Why does the leader wear those robes? What is this bread and juice? Who is Jesus? Is Jesus God? Is God Allah? The questions flow rapidly. We are in a time of spiritual searching. Our national magazines seem to have had more articles about religion in the last three or four years than they have had in many years. Although the attitudes of our society seem secular, we seem to have a compulsive interest in things related to religion, church and spirituality. As George Hunter III (2003) observes, there is "an unprecedented harvest of open, receptive, searching people who are looking for life, often in all the wrong places." This opens an enormous door for sharing the faith. We need to practice explaining difficult questions in a simple way. We need to be prepared to answer the hard questions. We need to think about the environments where we are given the opportunity to witness, and anticipate the questions and conversations that will happen in those settings.

Explaining can be such a helpful thing for people who are searching to understand the faith. We need to try our best to anticipate the kinds of questions that flow through an individual's mind as they search for meaning and truth in their life, as they search for explanation for what the church is, as they try to answer some of the difficult theological and behavioral questions of life. We need to be friends who can explain, will listen and want to help learn the answers to the ultimate questions of life. God has made us to be individuals who want answers, whether it's answers about what makes a particular part of nature function in the way that it does—why tornadoes come, why the snowflakes are so beautiful—or answers about behavior—why people behave in the ways they do, what are the phenomena that affect our attitudes of life, how are beliefs formed. All are answers that human beings search for throughout their lives. In the practice of everyday living, we want to know why our husband or wife disagrees or why they behave in a particular way; we want to know what our boss means by a memo or what a friend means in a casual comment. In the search for answers, we want someone to explain or to help us to find the answer.

One of the most exciting things about the Christian faith is finding answers, explanations, a way to explain the nature of God, the nature of human failure, the nature of life: How did creation begin? Why do people find themselves in conflict? What is freedom? We search for meanings about our ultimate direction: What is the goal of life? What is truth? How should we treat people? What's real satisfaction? What is heaven really like? How do I deal with my sin, my failures, my mistakes? These are questions we all ask. One of the key aspects of sharing the faith is to help people to find answers, to be able to explain. One of the biggest blockages to becoming a Christian is a failure to understand. As we have developed Christianity over the centuries, we have developed a lot of idiosyncrasies, ways of doing things that fit with certain groups of people–ways that have great meaning to various cultures–and, as they've been passed on, they become hard to understand. We need to help people understand. Probably some of the most difficult things we need to explain are our own negative behavior, the complicated theological questions or the tough questions about life and death. A part of sharing the faith is learning answers.

The front page headline of the Sunday paper was about a local Sunday school teacher who committed serious sexual indiscretions with some of the children in his class. As Erick read the paper that morning it was as if his three skeptical friends at work were asking him a million questions. He knew what they would say on Monday morning, the things they would ask or infer. He knew the jokes and sarcastic statements that would be said to him and others about this indiscretion. He also knew that this was an opportunity to explain what Jesus taught about morality and integrity, a chance to explain the standards of faith and the reality of our sinfulness. It was possibly a chance to open the door for his hardheaded sarcastic friends to hear the truth. He asked his wife if he could practice, so for a while on Sunday afternoon she played the role of his sarcastic friends while he practiced how to explain Christian ethics and the forgiveness of God in a way that would open an opportunity to really share what he believed was the truth. On Monday morning, just as he predicted, the sarcastic things were said and the criticism was almost delivered directly to him. But he was ready. Erick spoke with gentleness and clarity. He was not defensive but he was committed. The passion of his faith was not arrogant but a loving desire to let his friends know how Jesus' way helps us deal with our own frailty without giving up our ideals.

Perceptions of the Church

Many of the questions that we need to answer are questions about the Church. There are a multitude of perceptions and confusions about the nature of the Church today by people who are not involved in the Christian faith or the Church but also those who are involved in the Church. Dan Kimball, in his powerful book, *They Like Jesus But Not the Church*, lists six common perceptions of the Church today. Each one of these perceptions brings a multitude of questions for which we need to provide answers. Dan's six perceptions are 1) The church is an organized religion with a political agenda; 2) The church is judgmental and negative; 3) The church is dominated by males and oppresses females; 4) The church is homophobic; 5) The church arrogantly claims all other religions are wrong; and 6) The church is full of fundamentalists who take the whole Bible literally. Unless we are prepared to deal in some way with these confused perceptions of the Church, our ability to witness to the power of Christ will be blocked by the frustration of these perceptions. We need to train ourselves in dealing with the questions that are not always easy to answer.

An Opportunity to Explain

The skeptical, critical attitude toward Christianity does not always have to lead to defensiveness and frustration; it can be an opportunity for us to explain what the truth really is. We must keep our integrity clear, our spirit of love strong and be prepared to explain.

Finding answers together can be an enjoyable experience, an opportunity to build fellowship and understanding. Learning how to listen to each other in the midst of asking the questions, learning how to find the "ah-has" of life is so satisfying and so much fun. It can be a great opportunity to build fellowship and relationships in the midst of sharing our faith. One of the important aspects of a church's life should be helping people find answers: an in-depth Bible study, a review of systematic theology, a multi-week study of the basic truths of the teachings of Christ, an open discussion about the doctrines of the church, a study of historical practices of the faith–all these things can be exciting and great opportunities to learn and grow and build Christian friendship.

Catherine was one of the homeroom mothers. The other two moms who had time to help with school were also there that day. They had helped with several projects for the class, and they were waiting for the school day to end so they could take their third graders home. Mary Beth said to Catherine, "Are you a Charismatic?" Catherine knew that her two homeroom mother friends never mentioned church or faith and were probably agnostic or atheist. So when Mary Beth said, "Are you a Charismatic?" her first response was to be defensive, angry and give a sharp, cutting answer. But she had thought about this often since she had become friends with those two ladies. How would she share the faith? What words would work? When Mary Beth asked about the Charismatic movement, Catherine was surprised at the question, yet she had prepared herself and was ready to explain. The answer was simple, "No, I am not. The church we go to accepts the charismatic experience, but it is not a strong part of our denomination." Then she said, "You know, so many people are mixed up about how people worship, the differences between Charismatics, Pentecostals, Catholics and other denominations." Then she gave a simple answer about worship, personality styles and biblical examples. She concluded by talking about how important it is for us to find a comfortable way to get in touch with God. It was like Mary Beth was asking about her faith instead of Charismatics. She began to share her own spiritual journey and Sally, who had been quietly listening, chimed in with her own questions. The answers that were given were sensitive and caring, and in the end Catherine simply shared the truth about her life. As they talked together Catherine decided to lead. In a loving way she made the invitation. "Our church has a great program for kids. Adam really enjoys his class. If you are ever interested, I would love to have you visit our church." The invitation was simple, yet it opened a door. In future meetings they talked about church, and eventually both Mary Beth and Sally visited Catherine's church and became followers of Jesus.

Explain. The world needs to know.

Understand and Explain

As we seek to be able to explain better to our children, family, friends and acquaintances, we increase our own understanding and curiosity to find the answers. An important aspect of our spiritual growth is to learn how to answer the questions in a helpful way, not only for ourselves but for our families, our children, our friends, our casual acquaintances. Learning to be someone who thinks out their faith and can explain is one of the greatest gifts in terms of our personal growth. It can be our goal for any of us to become theologians. We should be thinkers as well as doers in the faith. Christians can be practical theologians and provide ways in which the church, pastors, theologians and individual members can explain things that are difficult. Topics like "Why do bad things happen to good people," "How should we pray," "How do I develop my spiritual life," "What is the Christian view of death," "How do we worship effectively" and "What is the meaning of the trinity" are just some of the topics that are no longer asked only during formal theological education. They have become common questions asked at the water cooler in the office. The Christian who has a clear, simple, systematic answer is able to share the faith and witness the power of the Gospel in a way that is open, receptive and helpful. In developing their ability to share, Christians need to become good theologians. Contemporary non-Christians will not understand about

Jesus Christ if we give them bad answers, judgmental positions or uneducated responses. Christians need to understand in the context of the contemporary culture that the answer may be complex rather than a simple solution. Often the answer may be that we don't know, but at least we have an intelligent explanation for our doubts and ambiguities.

Difficult Questions

Because of the complexity of some of the theological questions that some people may ask, it is certainly possible that individuals simply do not have a good answer or, that in attempting to explain, one finds that the answer is too complicated for typical discussion. We should be prepared to admit honestly and openly that we do not know or that we do not have the adequate definitions to explain. We should also be willing to ask known scholars, pastors and theological experts to help us. It is important to be honest in replying to a person who asks questions. Openly admit that it is difficult or complicated. In all of these discussions the focus should be upon the basic commitment to follow Christ, the basic issues of faith and the clear teachings of Jesus.

Because these questions are difficult, Christians who desire to find ways to witness effectively need to spend time finding, studying and practicing answers and explanations and thinking about appropriate vocabulary to use when explaining to skeptics. Make a goal of finding the answers that will work and practice sharing with friends and other committed Christians. Both techniques are helpful in developing those theological answers to tough questions.

Sometimes the answers are just difficult, complicated and hard to explain and understand. It is at this point that the committed Christian can simply admit the difficulty and focus upon the priorities of God's love, the simple teachings of Jesus, the Great

Commandments and the essence of the Christian faith without getting caught up in some of the difficult theological questions.

We Must Be Practical Christian Theologians

It has taken centuries for theologians to develop vocabulary for explaining some of the basic fundamental questions for life and death. Though we have great biblical information and powerful teachings of Jesus, there are still some questions that are not answered.

Dan Kimball expresses the need clearly as he states, "People today are open to Jesus, but the church needs to rethink how we come across to people on the outside. While we need to stand strong on what we believe and need not be ashamed of the Gospel in any way, we need to make sure we are presenting a biblical picture of the church and not perpetuating negative stereotypes. We need to offer an apologetic to common misperceptions" (Kimball, p. 250).

The challenge for all of us is to find the answers, to be able to be supportive of each other when the answers are hard or simply don't come. Part of being a Christian witness is to be able to love even when there are not clear, simple answers. In the midst of our doubts and ambiguities, we need to be strong about the things that we do believe in, to be clear about God's love for us, to be passionate about our love for others, to be enthusiastic about the good things we see in life, to celebrate the joys, the success and the victories that all of us find as we make the journey of life, and to be able to put words around these accomplishments and these opportunities is a task of explaining.

Sometimes we need to help people deal with their doubts and ambiguities. Why does a child die? Why does one cancer patient survive and another not? Why does our preference in music dictate so much understanding of a particular church's spiritual power? How do we teach values to our children in the midst of an extremely offensive secular environment? All these are questions we may need to deal with as we share the faith.

When we struggle to provide an answer for a friend who is not only looking for the answer but also looking for the meaning of life, we may need to begin a dialogue that includes sharing our personal story as a Christian. It might include an opportunity to invite or a chance to show how Christ has empowered your life. Explaining is not the end of witnessing; it is simply part of witnessing. Today it is an absolutely vital part. We need to be the kind of practical Christian theologians who can answer the questions facing our society today, whether they are asked by professionals or laity.

Questions for Discussion and Personal Reflection

1. Think of some of the tough questions you have had in your faith journey. List and discuss them.
2. Make a list of some of the tough questions being asked by people in our secular world.
3. Think of particular people you know who are in the midst of a faith journey. What are their questions?
4. Think of particular people who are atheists or antagonistic about God and faith. What are their questions?
5. Make a list of questions that are being asked in our society about the church, Christians and the Christian faith.
6. Share your positive experience in learning answers and sharing with others.
7. With the list of questions that you have summarized, begin to work on answers. How would you explain?

Chapter 9
Live

There is a disturbing lack of consistency in our society, and so many superficial approaches to life. People today long for someone who is authentic, real and honest. The most powerful witness that Christians have in today's society is living the faith. Following Jesus Christ clearly and regularly, both in the everyday aspects of our lives and through the crises, temptations and opportunities really makes a difference. Without authenticity, the explanation won't work. Some see the Christian as a self-righteous individual who is really a hypocrite. Christians need to recognize that they are being evaluated. We must exhibit integrity, responsibility, ethics and loving behavior. We must follow Jesus clearly. We are known by our behavior.

Hypocrisy

When Sam, the manager of his department who was a deeply devout Christian and regularly spoke openly about his faith, had an affair with his secretary, everyone in the office eventually knew about it. Sam's ability to witness was totally minimized. Not only was his ability to manage the department jeopardized, his failure became an evaluation of Christ's way. This is not an aspect of our faith that we should become compulsively fearful about and try to hide every imperfection of our own personal lives, but it is important that we realize that our lives are the example of Jesus Christ. How we live reflects the reality of Christ. Our bungling, our hypocrisy, our sins and our arrogance are blocks to non-Christians and we must deal with them as we seek to be a witness by how we live. It is because of this that the teachings of Jesus about caring, loving and helping become so important.

In the twenty-fifth chapter of Matthew, Christ made it clear that we are called to be those who help the least of these. Jesus taught in the tenth chapter of Luke that we are called to be like the Good Samaritan. The most powerful witness of our living is by serving, caring and helping. Meeting the needs of people around us is a way we can reflect the love of God through Jesus Christ. Some Christians feel that random acts of kindness are the way this can be done best. Don't take credit; don't manage what we do; just do little anonymous deeds of kindness. Certainly little acts of kindness are nice, helpful and Christ-like, yet only doing them randomly without purpose or meaning trivializes the message of Jesus Christ into some gimmicky behavior.

For people to see Christ through our acts of kindness, they should not be secretive or random but planned and clear. If people are to see Jesus Christ in your service, you need to be ready to make the witness that the reason you are here to help is that you know the power of God's love and want to share it with others. This is done not in an arrogant way, but rather a simple way of connecting kindness with the truth. Needs-based evangelism is a method that I have used to teach how ministry can be a powerful way to lead people to Christ. In this skeptical culture, it is the most powerful and effective way.

Show Christ

Tim's wife had filed for divorce. Their marriage had been terrible. They were totally incompatible and mean to each other, and the children were suffering under the pain of their dysfunctional marriage. They had been to counselor after counselor, and finally their marriage came apart. When that happened his life seemed to be totally broken. As ineffective as his family was, it was his identity. Now he was neither married nor regularly in touch with his kids. The divorce decree had put him in an odd situation and he felt like everything in his life was broken. He isolated himself for weeks. He used drugs and alcohol in excess. He said things about his ex-wife that should have never been said. He treated his children poorly. Then Tim happened by a church with a sign out front about a program to help divorced people. He was amazed that any church would care. He inquired about it, thinking it was probably some kind of program that would condemn all divorced people, but he found it was helpful, not condemning. He went to the workshop and classes, and he shared. The single people in that church showed love, compassion and acceptance and the church gave him a place to find community and self esteem again. The Christians he met loved him and were understanding and helpful. Tim saw Christ in them. Their example of such gentle care and understanding changed him. Their integrity, helpfulness and patience gave him a new understanding of life. When Tim stood at the altar of the church and confessed his faith in Jesus Christ it was because he had come to experience God's love. He said to the congregation that day, "Thank you for showing me what Jesus is really like. By loving me, forgiving me and helping me, you led me to Christ." He was baptized. His life was made full of new possibilities.

Live the Faith

Both the individual Christian and the church must live the faith. We must be authentic. As precious as the rituals of music and worship are, without the acts of living and caring, many of the things we do look self-centered, like some weird behavior of wannabe spiritual people. We will tell the story of Jesus best by our behavior. Jesus taught us clearly that what we are to do as Christians is let our behavior show the truth. The letter of James in the last part of the New Testament over and over emphasizes so clearly that faith without action simply is not alive. Jesus teaches the Sermon on the Mount in Matthew 5, 6 and 7 about behavior, about living the faith. The stories given in the twenty-fifth chapter of

Matthew, which is a chapter that really describes what the standards and guidelines for living the faith are, are about behavior, doing our best and helping those in need. Living the faith becomes the satisfaction and joy of being a Christian. It's the best way to witness to what we know is the truth.

False Signs

The way we live becomes the most obvious of the ways that we witness to our faith. One of the difficulties that Christians have is being unclear about what it means to live a Christian life. Over the centuries there have been a multitude of descriptions presenting standards of the Christian life. Often these present standards may be important, and yet they are not witnesses of faith. They become mechanical symbols that have no substance to the skeptical person.

The church has used all kinds of liturgies and behavioral symbols to indicate what it is to be a Christian: attending worship, membership in particular churches, attending certain kinds of rituals and activities. Though these may be important things for a Christian to do, they are ineffective in convincing the non-Christian that they should follow Jesus.

Regularly attending the Wednesday night prayer meetings of a particular church is a fine thing to do, and may be very satisfying. Yet other than an indication of a great sense of loyalty it does not convey the kinds of values that Jesus taught about in the Sermon on the Mount. The particular ways of dressing, particular garb of clergy and the designs of places of worship all have been important for church life yet these behaviors are not necessarily a positive witness to the non-Christian. So often they become the basis of the criticism of hypocrisy rather than the reality of following Jesus.

Real Witness in Love

In the tenth chapter of Luke, Jesus was in a discussion about what was necessary to inherit the kingdom. Out of that discussion biblical scholars agree that Jesus affirmed what have been called the Great Commandments. Jesus described what it is that a person does to follow Him: *"You shall love the Lord your God with all your heart, and with all your soul, and with all your strength, and with all your mind; and your neighbor as yourself"* (Luke 10:27 NASB). Jesus said if we would do this we would live. The standard then for witnessing through our living is: are we showing our love of God, are we showing our love of others and do we show that we love ourselves? These three dimensions of faith become a key to healthy living as well as healthy faith. These three rules–loving God, loving your neighbor and loving yourself–become the standards for what it is to be a Christian. It is in these acts of love that others will see God in us. The Great Commandments are a primary key to what it is to be a Christian.

Let Christ Be Seen in Your Life

Mary Ann's grandmother had lived so long under nursing care that most of her friends had died. The current ministers and other leaders of the church simply didn't know her. When it came time for words at her funeral to celebrate this lady's life, everything that the two presiding ministers said just seemed so inadequate to the family. Mary Ann was furious when the funeral was over. As the family gathered in the church parlor for the funeral dinner, after the minister gave a prayer for the meal and everyone had sat down to eat, she took her fork and clinked her glass as she stood to talk. She made it simple. She said she wasn't condemning the minister's words they had just heard at the funeral for they were appropriate and fine. Then she said, "He didn't know my mom. Mother was the most loving person I have ever known." As Mary Ann began telling stories about her mother, she was interrupted with laughter and interrupted with more stories. Her children, grandchildren and friends in the room began to tell the stories of love, of all the things that this woman had done for all of them and for anyone she met. Finally one teenage boy who seemed so bashful stood up and simply said in slow deliberate words, "My grandma taught me about Jesus, because she was Jesus." And then he sat down. Everybody knew what that meant. This lady had lived a life that was so loving and kind that God's love through Jesus shone in her and was reflected to everyone who knew her. That's what it is to witness by our life; so that people in knowing us will know Jesus.

Paul, wanting to make it clear, said all the law and all the prophets "are summed up in this word, *'You shall love your neighbor as yourself'*" (Romans 13:9 ESV). There is always a tendency for us to want to describe love in some very clear particulars. We want to make the rules about love. In an old movie, the punch line was, "Love means never needing to say, 'I'm sorry.'" It might seem like a beautiful rule in a romantic moment, and yet, there are sometimes love means you need to say you're sorry. Sometimes love, to be most meaningful, has to be expressed in clear terms. Other times, it's very general. I've found that the teachings of Charles Sheldon mentioned earlier in this book are so helpful at this point, for Sheldon's book, *In His Steps*, focused upon asking, "What would Jesus do?" It's built upon the idea that we would know Christ so well that, when we would be faced with a decision, we could ask, "What would Jesus do?" and it would be the most loving thing.

Love, finally, is situational. There are times when a child asks for an extension on their allowance and the loving answer is no; there are other times when it is yes. It depends on the whole situation. This is not a way of making excuses about responsibility; it's being appropriate and loving in a way that is understood as really loving. Certainly, there are principles within our society having to do with justice, human rights and dignity; there are times in our society when love has to do with helping people in need, unselfish giving and acts of compassion. There are times when love is planned, programmed and organized and times when it is spontaneous. The important thing is that we do our best to be the most loving people possible and, in doing that, though we may be misunderstood at times, we will most often clearly witness to the power of Jesus Christ.

Questions for Discussion and Personal Reflection

1. Consider several of the ways that the hypocrisy of Christians has blocked people from coming to understand and accept Jesus Christ.
2. Give several examples of how someone's life as a Christian influenced you personally.
3. In the Great Commandment Jesus said we are to love our neighbor as ourselves. How does that kind of love provide a witness for the effectiveness of the Christian faith?
4. Spend a few moments in prayer, honestly talking to God about your faults, mistakes and things you do that might block others from knowing the love of Christ.
5. List projects, actions and behavior that can be a positive life influence on others to follow Jesus Christ.

Chapter 10
Lead

Lynn was going through chemotherapy. He was discouraged and his doctor suggested that he attend some kind of support group. His wife knew of a church that had such a group so Lynn reluctantly went to one of the meetings. He found that the support group was very helpful. It was made up of people who were either going through cancer treatment, had already finished cancer treatment or had loved ones with cancer. They were people who understood. They had struggled with some of the same issues he had. He came to love the group; it was so accepting and they had a good time together. He finished his series of chemotherapy, and, at the next meeting, he thanked the group for all they had done for him. He told them they had set such a great example and acted with such love that it had made a difference. Then he paused and said, "You saved my life."

The other members of the group were of several categories. The majority of the group members were not members of John Street Church where the meetings took place. They had come because they needed a group and wanted some help. Since they formed the support group, more than half had become active in the church. More importantly they found a new experience of Christ in their lives. Two of them had once been devoted Christians, and they recaptured what they had lost. Several were deeply committed Christians who were still active in a church, and went to the support group because they believed in what was happening. Four had never been to church and really didn't know what church was about. As they worked together in the cancer support group and attended worship with their new friends, their lives changed and they made the decision to become committed Christians.

The support group had been created by a few individuals who understood the need and also understood it would be a way to lead hurting people to the healing power of God. All of them had been involved with cancer. Most had gone through the treatments and were in some way cancer free, and two of them were spouses of cancer victims. Because they knew what faith could mean and what Jesus taught, they were passionate about the group. When their pastor told them about a book called *Needs-Based Evangelism*, they laughed and said, "We could write that book," for that was what they were doing.

The night Lynn thanked everyone and spoke about his own spiritual journey, Tony knew he had to lead. He had to help his friend, Lynn, understand what the next step was. So after Lynn finished speaking, Tony told his own story about battling cancer. Some had already heard that story, but it was such a sweet, honest, humble story that it was refreshing to everyone that night. Tony said what had made a difference for him was his personal relationship with Jesus Christ as his Lord and Savior. He took a few minutes to simply explain what that commitment meant, and then he repeated what others had often said. This group was created by active Christian church leaders to share the healing power of God. He explained further that they were not forcing or pressuring anyone who hadn't committed their lives to Christ to make that decision, but he went on and said, "If you do, when you are ready, I am here to help you." After he finished, the conversation went on about faith and healing.

As the meeting ended, Lynn and his wife walked out toward the vestibule of the church and Tony followed. With them were two other church members who had been part of the group for a long time. To a casual observer it looked like there were five people leaving the meeting to go to their cars and leave the church, but that's not what happened. Tony knew that now was the time to speak to Lynn. As Lynn approached the front door of the church Tony called out his name and asked him to wait a moment. When he stepped up to his friend he put his arm around his shoulder and expressed his thanks for what he had said that night. Then Tony led. He simply said to his friend, "I know you have been coming to church from time to time. I know from what you said tonight that you are becoming a person of faith." Then Tony asked Lynn if he had ever accepted Christ as his Lord and Savior. Tony then asked if he wanted to clearly make this commitment in his life and if he wanted to be baptized. By this time they were standing in the parking lot and Lynn was crying. His wife put her arms around him and began crying too. The two other church members caught up with Tony and Lynn and as they stood in the parking lot it became a giant hug fest. There were tears everywhere. Lynn said, "Thank you." Then he coughed and said, "I have been trying to have enough courage to ask one of you church people how to do it. What I mean is how do you give your life to Jesus Christ? How do you become a part of the church? I have seen people in front of the altar, but I haven't understood what it is all about and I want to be a Christian. I was raised in a totally secular home. We probably only went to church a few times at Christmas and Easter. I don't even understand about all the technicalities about being a Christian. How much does it cost to join the church, what are the dues? I don't know whether you need to examine me or test me. I don't know anything but I know I have found Jesus Christ in my life through this support group and I want to commit my life."

Tony gulped and he realized he better explain it clearly. So he said, "Would you like to go to the Corner Café and have a piece of pie and talk about all this?" Lynn and his wife immediately said, "Yes."

The other two said, "We will join you too." For the next hour these three committed Christians led Lynn and his wife to a new understanding. They committed their lives to Christ.

Leadership Is Our Imperative

In the process of being a Christian witness we must learn how to lead. The old evangelistic model of the hell, fire and brimstone preacher scaring everybody to death and telling them to come to the front and give their life to Christ was effective in its time. But the arrogance and self-righteousness of the old style is not the style of leading someone to Christ that works well today. We must understand as a Christian that leading is imperative. We must invite, encourage, direct and support others as they become Christians.

The goal of our leadership is to help someone to become a fully devoted follower of Jesus Christ. Though sometimes it may seem hard, this must be our natural way of responding to people who don't know Christ. Our desire must be built upon our inner commitment to Christ to do what He has called us to do, knowing how much each of us need to find this relationship with God through Jesus Christ. The way in which leadership is done is most important; certainly inviting, in whatever way it is directed, is so important–inviting to an event, inviting someone to the worship service, inviting someone to accept Christ, inviting someone to be a part of a discipleships group–all are important aspects of our leadership. Too often, the sign on the door, an announcement in the bulletin or a few words said at the pulpit are our ways of handling the invitation. There is much, much more to it, and it must be seen as a part of our life as an individual Christian. The invitation and action need to be based on encouragement; in our society today, our need to be positive and helpful is so important. Certainly, there are reasons for us to be concerned about the results of our highly secular society, the lack of morality and integrity, the continual actions of unkindness, self-centeredness and meanness throughout our society remind us of how important it is for us to lead people to Christ, point our responsibilities of leadership and the dangers of a very secular society. At the same time, the most positive tool is to point out the advantages of following Christ, to be an encourager.

The word "direct" is a simple way to remind us to keep on target. Sometimes, in the midst of the criticism of our present society, we are afraid to step out in a more direct kind of way; we are afraid of being called arrogant, insincere or manipulative, but, without our being direct, nothing happens. So many times, our leadership lacks a conviction or intentionality. We invite people to church, worship, parties, special events or a support group, but we don't follow through by inviting them to accept Christ, grow spiritually or find the joy of discipleship. It seems so ironic because we have found that joy and power and yet we're hesitant to lead and be direct. So many times, I have found that the attendee of our worship service or participant in our ministry is confused when we don't follow up with the invitation; we seem like we are hypocrites as we invite to attend but don't invite to belong. Numerous times, I've been told by people who were visiting, "Why didn't you ask me? I've been surprised that no one was direct and encouraged me to become a Christian." We may be afraid to offend, be misunderstood or seem pushy or arrogant, and yet, what we have to share is so precious, why should we hesitate? We can be direct and still act with love. We can be direct and still be patient and understanding. We can be direct and not be judgmental or mean.

The final characteristic of this leadership that is so important is to be supportive. When Paul described us as the body of Christ, He described us in terms of our unity, the fact that we work together as a team, that we are not alone and separate, but we're together. This means that, for a new Christian, follower of Christ, disciple or church member, we need to provide the support, help, information and love that are needed. It is easy for a new Christian to get lost in the maze of organizational life of any church or misunderstand the message of Jesus when it's interpreted so many ways by so many churches; it's easy for the new Christian to become discouraged when they don't have clear information and a clear understanding of what it means to follow Jesus. Our task is not only to lead in the beginning of the journey, but to be there and provide support all the way through the journey. The irony is that as we do provide that leadership support, eventually that new Christian becomes an experienced, mature follower of Christ and oftentimes they're the ones who give us the support in our difficult moments.

Lead by Inviting

Much of the evangelism talk in contemporary mainline churches today is about hospitality, being a friendly church. We have "Bring a Friend" Sundays, nametag boards and sign-up sheets. Effective churches have a cordial way in which they welcome visitors. They have found all kinds of techniques of hospitality that really work. One of the first and most practiced ways of leading someone to Christ is to invite them to attend. There are two characteristics of that invitation that make the difference whether it works or not.

The first is to build a warm, loving relationship with the individual you are inviting. Christian leadership is more than a quick invitation or a post card in the mail; it is effective when it is part of a loving friendship or relationship. Too often we use mailers or media ads and forget the power of the church members. At our church, the first time Mark invited Sue and Will to church was after they had spent several weeks together in a support group and developed a strong friendship. That relationship of love is the power of the living Christ. We must lead with love.

Second, we invite with information. People want to have answers to their questions. What? Why? What time? Where? How long? What do I do? Information is essential for Christ's love to be experienced. People are not comfortable with ambiguity. Effective invitations are clear invitations.

Local churches need to understand that invitational evangelism does not work unless we have something to invite the individual to.

Simply asking someone to come to church is usually not enough; there needs to be a reason. Secular people ask why; they want to know what is going to happen at church. Effective invitation usually comes out of a good relationship.

Ann and Jill were at the singles party the church was holding. Ann said to Jill, "I would love for you to come and attend church with me this Sunday." The answer she received from her friend was typical for a person who had not been to church in 12 years. Jill asked, "Why; what is going on?" Ann said, "We are having church, and I would love to have you come." Her new friend said, "But really, is there anything special?" Ann said, "Well no, just the preaching, singing and they are really friendly people." Her new friend said, "Is there anything..." and she paused because she was looking for an invitation, a reason to break her pattern of never attending church. The inviter needs a reason for the invitation. The leader can say we are having a special gospel quartet, the pastor is starting a new sermon series on developing good relationships, the youth are doing a special drama or the mayor is going to speak this Sunday and give her testimony of faith. The church needs to help the inviters by having invitational worship. It doesn't have to be gimmicky; it just needs to be real and authentic, with a clear quality based on real need. Something worth inviting people to see and experience.

Lead With Hospitality

All the standards of good hospitality must be part of that invitation, including someone to greet them at the church and no obnoxious or embarrassing situations created for the visitor. Some churches ask all the visitors to stand or, in smaller congregations, to stand and introduce themselves. Many visitors are not comfortable with standing in a strange church and introducing themselves. Many visitors don't attend church because they don't want to be embarrassed. If they do attend, they won't identify themselves as a visitor.

Lloyd had attended the church for years. He never once signed the attendance book; he never attended Sunday school and he never said anything to anyone. He always sat in the back row. Then he began to give. The finance officer of the church and the pastor were confused, who was this new person giving so regularly? They checked the rolls over and over. They had no record of this person ever visiting because Lloyd wanted no overt hospitality. He eventually recommitted his life, joined the church and became a leader. At the beginning he simply needed the privacy.

Hospitality must also be done for the gregarious person who is looking for a friendly church. Some people want to be greeted, given the brochures as well as a cup of coffee and a mug to take home. Yet for other visitors this is the wrong way to show hospitality.

All of this reminds us that people are different and the ways of leading people to Christ have to be varied. We must not be closed-minded about certain techniques but continually be open to new ideas of how to show this love and compassion without offending or frightening the visitor.

In a practical way, the concept of sensing another's needs is the most productive way to build a relationship and establish communications. General invitation to worship or Sunday school can be most important, but the particular invitation that shows how Christ meets our particular needs is what makes a difference.

Alice was a single mom and her child was in the church's day-care program. She was struggling with finances. Alice hadn't been to church since she was in the seventh grade and then she only went occasionally because her boyfriend belonged to the church. After they broke up she never went back to church until the day she enrolled her child in the daycare center. She became acquainted with the daycare leaders and other parents who were active members of the church and thought about going back to church for her daughter's sake. However she could never think of a time or reason to go. One day one of the other moms told her about a church support group for parents of toddlers. It would cover the child's developmental stage and what to expect in kindergarten. When the mom asked Alice if she would like to join the group, she admitted that this was something she desperately needed. She went to the support group and became friends with several committed Christians from the church. She had been given a reason to go to the church, although she still only came to the church for the Tuesday evening support group. Later she noticed in the church newsletter an announcement about a sermon series on faith and families, and it even mentioned single parents. When one of her new friends invited her to come to hear this new series she said yes and eventually her life was changed.

We need to lead by inviting. We need to be aggressive but in a gentle, sweet kind of way. Think of all the ways to invite people to the church. Invitational worship and invitational events are significant ways that a church needs to plan in order to give the opportunity for church members to invite others to the church and to Christ. Invitational evangelism works when there is a reason for secular people to break out of their negative feelings towards the church and attend with an open mind. A majority of the time the key to successful invitational worship and invitational events is having them meet real, honest needs.

Leading to Jesus

Some would think the hardest part of the "TELL" model is leading a person to actually accept Jesus as Lord and Savior. We can organize invitational events, we can put together hospitality, we can be at the door to greet, we can invite our friend to a concert but asking them point blank to accept Jesus Christ is hard for some people. We give all kinds of reasons why, having to do with not wanting to be arrogant or obnoxious, not being sure about all the potential questions or just simply not having a personality that make it easy for us to share or invite. But even though it might be hard we need to spend time thinking about how we can lead people to Christ and how we can help them make the decision. That leadership might be in any kind of setting. It may mean leading someone in your family, someone at your office, an acquaintance of a club or group you belong to or an individual that has been coming to some kind of needs-based evangelism program.

Finally we have to ask the person to become a Christian, to accept Christ as their Lord and Savior. As a college student a long time ago I worked hard to raise the money to go to college, and, after being at the University of Oklahoma for a year and an half, I had to drop out because I was broke. Eventually I found a whole series of jobs from driving a truck to selling insurance, but the biggest period of time I spent selling Fuller brushes. Fuller is a company that specialized in door-to-door selling where the sales person would carry a bag in and ring doorbells to tell the individuals what products we carried and explain the benefits. This worked back when people greeted and spoke to people at the door. It worked in a time when people were not so skeptical. For me the hardest part of selling Fuller brushes was asking someone to buy the product. My manager scolded me over and over; he always told me I would never make a living and save money to go back to college unless I learned how to close the deal. "You have to ask for the sale," he taught.

So many Christians are afraid to "close the deal." They are unsure about asking for the commitment. The reality is that we will not be able to lead people to Christ in many occasions unless we take the leadership role. Certainly some people will make that decision as they sit in worship on a Sunday morning. Certainly other individuals will become a part of a needs-based evangelism program such as a support group for parents of pre-adolescence or widow/widowers fellowship. Many people listen to the preaching, read their own Bible and make a decision by themselves with no encouragement and no leading by someone else. This is great, yet, so many others will never make the decision unless they are led. Our own commitment to Christ must be the empowering passion that helps us to make the invitation; not for them to just attend a service but to give their life to Christ. We must learn how to say it in a way that is not obnoxious, but natural for us.

We need to find new approaches for encouraging others. There is not a set of four or five questions that you should ask. Effectiveness in actually leading someone to Christ has to do with your passion, creativity and personal commitment. You have to use all the techniques you know; consequently it would be great if we had regular practice sessions in church life to rehearse communicating with others about Christ. It would be great if we would organize the kind of training that produces flexible, adaptable invitation not some kind of canned conversation. While I was a Fuller brush salesman the manager eventually taught me a little sales pitch that I memorized and said over and over to the people at the door as I presented the Fuller brush products. That might work to sell brushes, but it won't work to sell Jesus Christ. There is no repetitive, simplistic way to lead someone to Christ. It is based upon relationships, hurts, needs and feelings. We need to be ready to lead in many different situations and many different ways.

Principles

The principles of leading an individual to Christ need to be learned and remembered. These principles are a part of our commitment and passion for Christ. They are principles that must be dealt with by the individual making the commitment. The individual needs to understand that he is a sinner who needs God's forgiveness and help. We need to remember that *"God so loved the world that he gave his only Son, so that everyone who believes in Him may not perish but may have eternal life"* (John 3:16). This understanding of God's love, sometimes called God's grace by theologians, is an understanding that God forgives us, loves us and cares for us. It is to understand that we as Christians believe that God approaches us not as naughty troublemakers in His beautiful world but as His own children that He loves and cares for desperately. To understand that this is shown through Jesus Christ is the key to making the decision to follow Christ. It is out of that understanding of love and grace that we can accept His way exhibited in Christ. We need to confess our sins, admit we have done wrong and repent. Be sorry. This becomes easy as we accept Jesus as our Lord and Savior, a Savior whose death is a sign of God's love, a Savior who is our Lord, our leader. Once we commit our lives and follow Him as Lord, our lives are changed for the good. We receive the gift of God's guidance, the Holy Spirit or Spirit of God. We are empowered to make our lives and the world build on the teaching of Jesus, which is love. This is a joyful experience! This is a deeply satisfying experience, to understand and believe that God loves us despite our faults and that we have a possibility to live a better life, that we can be helpful, caring; that, in the midst of our hurt and our suffering, in the midst of our anger and bewilderment, God loves us, helps us, heals us and encourages us to be loving, not out of a sense of anger toward us but as a deep compassionate love for us.

We need to trust in God's beautiful love for us and His care for those that we seek to share with, and we need to believe that God's personality, His Spirit is present influencing the whole situation. We may try our best to witness right, share the faith and be a good example, but finally, we need to trust that God will take our effort and make it be fruitful.

As we seek to share the faith, so often we feel that we somehow have the absolute imperative to convince the individual to change their ways. They must accept Christ and become a devoted follower. Oftentimes we push and shove and worry and fret. Jesus loved to describe life in terms of growth. Whether it is the parable of the sower or His use of metaphors having to do with planting, growth and harvesting, we must understand that God is active in all that we do. It may be the farmer who plants the seed in the ground and provides assistance with water and fertilizer, but it is God who provides the sun. It is God who puts the genetic possibility into the seed. It is God who grows the plant. We must attempt to share the faith while trusting that God will use our attempts. God will take our words, our example, our acts of really helping and showing kindness, and bring fruit. God is asking us to join Him. Bring the planters, the sowers, the inviters, the leaders, the explainers and tellers, and God will do the growth. The work of God's Holy Spirit is active in all that we do. One of the keys to sharing the faith is to trust; trust in God's ability to work with every circumstance and every situation.

It is in the prayer that Jesus makes His request clear: *"Thy kingdom come; thy will be done."* To ask and to trust that God will bring the fruit, bring the result is the final piece that a Christian has in doing their best.

Tell

Questions for Discussion and Personal Reflection

1. What are other ways that we can provide leadership to people making a commitment to Christ?
2. Make a list of the ways in which we practice Christian hospitality individually and as a church.
3. What are some types of hospitality that you have done, can do or should do?
4. What are the words you would use to help someone to make a decision to commit their life to Christ?
5. What are some words you should not use to help someone to make a decision to commit their life to Christ?
6. How does the church lead people to make a commitment to Christ?
7. Pray that God will give you opportunities to lead people to Christ.

Chapter 11
Workable Evangelism

Although I have outlined steps, procedures, ideas, priorities in sharing your faith and leading new people to Jesus Christ, there is a concept that must be celebrated above all the ideas, instructions or coaching of this book or any book on personal evangelism. That concept is effectiveness. We need to do what works! Just as personalities are different, for God has made us all different, so we share our faith differently. As we seek to show our faith, oftentimes we're trapped in our own conclusions, which are that "you should witness my way" or, "you should witness in the way that my church, my group or my family share the faith." Certainly, there is some validity in our own testimony of what works, and I pray that the words of this book give each of you good instruction, helpful methodologies and effective evangelism techniques; however, all of us must realize that it depends on the individual and what works for the individual. It is the task of each of us, as we experience the power of Jesus Christ in our own lives, to share our faith in a way that is most natural for us and most effective for others. It's so easy in a church to decide that our way of doing church is the way of doing it in the church. Some people love traditional music, and it's the only kind of worship that is meaningful for them, but others like a variety of different music styles. One style is preferred by one group and another is preferred by different group.

It was a small rural church in Oklahoma. Three members were left, and they sat together on one occasion to decide what to do with their church. They decided that, instead of closing the doors, they would open the doors on a "cowboy church." The music and the liturgy was cowboy style. Such a church experience might be obnoxious to you, but it was effective for them; the church grew to over 200 in average attendance and new people were led to Christ.

We must understand that effectiveness in leading people to Christ is our goal. Whether it's cowboy style, Contemporary, Gospel, Traditional, High Church, Low Church–the priority is Jesus Christ. That was never clearer to me than when the great evangelist, Harry Denman, visited the town where I served as pastor.

In the history of Christianity, there are many who are known as great evangelists–people who set an example for all of us in how to share the faith, people who were so effective that the history of the Church was affected by their ministry. Their stories–radically different and yet very much the same–illustrate this principle of effective evangelism. The first is my story of a personal experience with Harry Denman. These stories help us to understand. The second is a story of a Bible study group that I participated in, where a woman named Carolyn helped us understand the practical way, the power of Paul's evangelistic methodology.

Sometimes, to understand something, we have to experience it, see it, hear it and feel it. The story on the following pages is the story of the most famous evangelist in the Methodist Church–a man named Harry Denman who lived from 1893 to 1976. He became head of the Board of Evangelism of the Methodist Church and set an example for evangelism that was to impact the Church significantly. He was quoted frequently and remembered by the old timers of our churches as "Mr. Evangelism." I had lunch with Harry once. This is the story.

Harry Denman's Model

I first served as pastor in a Methodist church when I was a junior in college. I served that first rural church in northern Oklahoma for two and a half years. Since I did not have enough money to go to seminary without working, I completed my seminary education while serving as pastor in Hennessey, Oklahoma. My first church job out of seminary was associate pastor at First United Methodist Church in Tulsa, Oklahoma, where I worked as youth director and director of evangelism. During all of these eight and a half years of ministry, I was involved in evangelism. The churches I served grew. Yet it was in a small restaurant in Stillwater, Oklahoma, that I came to understand evangelism most clearly!

While I was pastor of a new church in Stillwater, a speaker from the Board of Evangelism in Nashville, Tennessee, was in town to speak at my church. I was excited. Harry Denman had come to town! And there we were, sitting together at a small restaurant in the college town of Stillwater. I had heard the stories that Harry would witness anywhere, at any time. He was always sharing Jesus Christ. I knew the stories of how he would witness to the waitresses at restaurants, and there I was with him at a restaurant as the waitress came up. I waited. What would happen? Were the stories right?

Harry had a smile on his face all the time; he was filled with energy and love for everyone. He quickly began to talk to the waitress in a way that made her comfortable. He asked questions, drawing her into a relaxed conversation. He asked about her job, her family and her life. He told her about his life and his faith. In casual conversation he came to appreciate and understand her and her situation. In a moment I saw the great evangelist break down the barriers, share in a candid way who Christ is and invite her to become Christ's follower. Harry was a master at understanding people. He lived the faith and knew the words. He was genuine, honest and a man of integrity. I had that one special moment of seeing him share the faith in Jesus Christ with a waitress as she served our food. She said she would take him up on the invitation so he got her name and gave it to me to follow up on, for he was leaving town that very day. To tell the truth, I was scared to death to be sitting next to such a great evangelist. I don't know what I was afraid of—maybe that he would ask me to witness or speak some magic words that would bring in the kingdom of God at that moment. But he just did what was natural for him. He shared love, joy and possibility with a young woman in the midst of her work for that day. He understood her, and he invited her to know Jesus. It wasn't obnoxious, arrogant, self-righteous, judgmental or mean. It was just the loving Gospel of Jesus being shared by somebody who knew Christ.

After that day, I never thought I could be like Harry. I couldn't come up with the kind of beautiful words, humorous stories, delightful laugh or spontaneous conversation. I was more controlled and methodical in the way that I operated my life. But after seeing what he did, I want to dedicate this book to the memory of a man who made evangelism natural. I pray that everyone who reads these chapters will find sharing and witnessing for Christ to be natural and really fun.

Practical Principles

In the story of Henry Denman, there are some things that were clear to me when we finished. One, because I was so in awe of him, I thought at first he was almost magical in terms of leading people to Christ. Now, years later, I understand that it is not that Harry was magical; it's that he was effective. So what did he do that made such a difference? The following are my reflections upon that lunch with Harry a long time ago.

First, Harry wanted to share the faith. It was natural for him; it was almost second nature. He believed so much in Jesus Christ and so much in sharing that experience that he had to do it. Many of us today have become such skeptics about lots of things. We're afraid; we're unsure. We have become unsure about how to share the faith. We have become bashful Christians, afraid of what someone would think, say or do, so we don't say or do anything. Harry was not afraid. He wanted to tell people about Jesus. It was evident in knowing him, talking to him and being aware of his career; that's who he was and that's what he believed. If we are going to be people who can share the faith, we must have that same kind of conviction about the truth that is Jesus Christ—that it is a great story, what the world needs and what we live our lives based upon. We've got to share it!

Secondly, it was clear that Harry cared about everyone he met. When Jesus said, "Love your neighbor as yourself," Harry did it. He loved everybody. He was not arrogant, self-righteous or overbearing. He just cared. The conversation with the waitress at the little restaurant in Stillwater was not some kind of memorized conversation listing four points or three steps; it was just him caring about that woman. The questions he asked, long before he said anything about Jesus, were simple questions about her life and her job. You knew from the moment that he began to respond to her that he cared; he wasn't overbearing or pushy. It was an example of one Christian meeting another human being and caring in the same way that God cares for all of us. Because most of us don't do that very well, it seemed amazing, unusual and miraculous. But it was just love. It was like First Corinthians 13 or Romans 12 was being acted out in front of my eyes: patient, kind, not jealous or boastful, not arrogant or rude. Somehow, we need to learn how to care.

Thirdly, he listened. He listened with a passion. He caught the tone of her voice, inferences in what she said and references to her child at home. He paid attention. In another part of the book, I mentioned Meredith Wilson's play, *The Music Man*, where the salesmen sang, "You've Got to Know the Territory." Harry got to know her in a few moments because he listened so well. Many times, we don't listen to our children, acquaintances or best friend. We're so busy talking, persuading and trying to get our own way that we don't listen. Listening is an absolute necessity for sharing the faith.

Fourth, Harry was clear about the invitation. He asked her questions about whether or not she went to church and was a

135

Christian. He asked those questions not in a condemning way but as a part of the conversation that he had already established as she waited on us and took our breakfast order. In a short period of time, he had developed such a rapport that the questions about her faith were not obnoxious or probing but just questions from someone who was interested. How he inquired and then invited was so natural; there wasn't a place for an argument about whether or not the church was relevant or if they spoke in tongues or use a formal liturgy. It was just one human being saying to another human being, "Would you like to know Jesus better? Would you like to go to church?" Somehow, we need to capture that innocence in making the invitation. So many times, it's so complicated and qualified that we never get the invitation made in a way that's genuine. It sounds more like we're selling tickets to some performance rather than inviting someone to know Jesus.

Finally, Harry sealed his sharing with a clear follow-up. He found out her name and phone number, introduced me to her, told her who I was and what I did and explained to her that I would be giving her a call about some details of the church. Under some circumstances, that might have been quite fast and very invasive, but with all the love, listening, compassion and caring Harry showed, it wasn't inappropriate; it just made sense. Too many times, we don't follow up in evangelism; we don't make the follow-up phone call; we don't share the name with someone else at the church; we don't check on their friends or family or other references in their life; we just send a volley of invitation shots across the bow of someone else's ship and sail away, feeling that we've done our duty. The story of Harry Denman in the little restaurant for breakfast in Stillwater, Oklahoma, many years ago may seem like an unimportant story in the midst of a book on witnessing for Jesus Christ, but it is a real-life example that taught a young pastor a valuable lesson on evangelism, and I believe can teach all of us today.

Effective

That is my story of Harry Denman. When I sat with him at a café preparing to order our food I wondered: Would he do what everybody said he would do? When the waitress came to the table and asked about our order Harry began to talk about the food, then he began to talk about her and then he talked about Christ. He was sweet and gentle. He loved. Having heard the stories about Harry witnessing to waitresses and waiters, I thought I might have been embarrassed or shocked. What he did was simple. It was his way, and it was effective.

I asked him after we left the restaurant, "Harry, do you really think it makes a difference to witness to the waitress?" In my young arrogance I was skeptical about the effectiveness of a short conversation while you are ordering a plate of food. Harry said, "I'm planting the seeds. God will grow the fruit. My job is to plant. I am not worrying about the fruit, I trust that the Spirit of God was present in everything I said and did at that restaurant."

That answer seemed much too simple to me as a young theologian. That was a kind of cop out for an old guy. As I have become an old guy, I now realize that Harry was telling the truth. Sure we have to take responsibility and share in a way that is as effective as possible. We need to share in a loving, kind way and be as wise as we possibly can. But we need to remember our witness is for the work of God's kingdom. We need to trust that God hasn't given us this task without promising the help, the fruit and the possibility. Certainly there are times when nothing happens, when our efforts seem to have been a waste. Yet maybe what we said or what we did was a small picture in the whole landscape of ways God was trying to influence and lead that person to a new life. God will bring the results. Trust.

As you study ways of reaching new people for Christ and relate to their environment and culture, it is imperative that you consider foremost what works, whether it's an old method or a new method. Whether it's a vocabulary to relate to the postmodern generation or the GI generation, we are called to share the Gospel in a way that is effective. In my story with Harry Denman, he shared the faith in a way that made a difference to a waitress. I may never be able to do the kind of personal evangelism that Harry Denman was famous for, but I can do evangelism that works with my personality, my community and my situation. So it is for each of us. Be effective.

Paul's Workable Evangelism

We were sitting in a Bible study studying the book of Acts and reflecting upon the experiences of those early Christians as they parallel our lives today. We had read Acts 17:22–34, and we were discussing Paul's remarks to the people of Athens about faith in Christ. This passage reads:

> *Paul then stood up in the meeting of the Areopagus and said: "People of Athens! I see that in every way you are very religious. For as I walked around and looked carefully at your objects of worship, I even found an altar with this inscription: TO AN UNKNOWN GOD. So you are ignorant of the very thing you worship—and this is what I am going to proclaim to you. The God who made the world and everything in it is the Lord of heaven and earth and does not live in temples built by human hands. And he is not served by human hands, as if he needed anything. Rather, he himself gives everyone life and breath and everything else. From one man he made all the nations, that they should inhabit the whole earth; and he marked out their appointed times in history and the boundaries of their lands. God did this so that they would seek him and perhaps reach out for him and find him, though he is not far from any one of us. 'For in him we live and move and have our being.' As some of your own poets have said, 'We are his offspring.' Therefore since we are God's offspring, we should not think that the divine*

being is like gold or silver or stone—an image made by human design and skill. In the past God overlooked such ignorance, but now he commands all people everywhere to repent. For he has set a day when he will judge the world with justice by the man he has appointed. He has given proof of this to everyone by raising him from the dead." When they heard about the resurrection of the dead, some of them sneered, but others said, "We want to hear you again on this subject."

At that, Paul left the Council. Some of the people became followers of Paul and believed. Among them was Dionysius, a member of the Areopagus, also a woman named Damaris, and a number of others.

Principles

As the group discussed the story of Paul at Areopagus, Carolyn joined in the conversation and pointed out how clearly what Paul did in a polytheistic world in Athens is a model for us today. She reminded us that, first, Paul began with an affirmation to the people of Athens. As he stood with them on Areopagus, a hill that was known as a place of debate and discussion of philosophy, religion and current affairs, Paul complimented them on their religiosity. He pointed out the statues to various deities.

Second, in the midst of affirming and understanding, he commented on a particular idol to an unknown god. He said he knew the answer to who that unknown god was. So often, as we listen to our friends get involved in discussion of religion, we don't listen to their real questions; we have memorized answers and responses, without understanding where our friend is. Paul understood the people of Athens like we should understand our friends who are searching for the unknown God.

Third, Paul gave an answer that was relevant to the people he was speaking to; his answer was given in words of philosophy, words of the culture of the time. He spoke in a way that they could understand. It is easy for us to use religious clichés and preconceived doctrinal statements to explain points that our secular friends do not understand at all. Paul put it in a way that it could be understood and related to their culture, time and situation. So we must share our faith in a way that it is understandable and makes sense to the people we're sharing with.

Fourth, he then ended with a simple statement about Christ, an explanation of the nature of God, the nature of life; in a few words, he commented on the whole human struggle and pointed out that Jesus Christ is the answer.

Fifth, the Scripture said some mocked, but others joined him and believed. So often in our struggle to share the faith, we want 100 percent without realizing that God works with people differently; some will join and some will mock, but all will hear. The story is beautiful.

That night, as Carolyn shared with us an interpretation of the story of Paul at the Areopagus, we realized it is an effective model for all of us. There are lots of books written about how to share your faith, and the book of Acts may be one of the best.

We must find the ways to do evangelism that work for us, the situation, our personalities and the characteristics of the individuals who are listening. Too many times, we approach sharing the faith with a sense of rigorous rules that have to be followed. However, our goal should be to follow the spiritual rules of effectiveness, doing what we need to do that works to help someone find the power of Jesus Christ in their life. The purpose of this book is to provide as many ideas as possible to help the Church become more effective in reaching people for Christ. Much has changed in our society; much has changed in the Church, but the call to lead people to Christ is just as much an imperative as it ever was. In a sense, the chapters in the book need to be written by each of us in our experience of sharing the faith. We need to do what works and helps a person come to Christ. Harry Denman's way was one way; Bob Pierson's way is slightly different. Paul approached it with the Greeks in a somewhat different way. Each of us wants to do what works. So it may be with each person who reads this book—may each person be committed to finding the way to tell the story that works, that really leads a person to find the power of Jesus Christ in their life. That is workable evangelism.

Questions for Discussion and Personal Reflection

1. Share one of your experiences in witnessing or leading someone to Christ that was meaningful to you.
2. Discuss and reflect upon the different ways that people witness and how effective or ineffective the different ways are now.
3. Reflect upon the story of how Harry Denman made his methodology work so well and how it relates to your journey.
4. Spend time in prayer asking for God's direction in being effective as you share the faith.
5. Read again the story of Paul in Athens and ascertain your own meaning and directions out of his example of evangelism.

Chapter 12
Trust God

Those of us who organize, manage and do the work of the church often fail to be responsible. We try but don't finish or even start. We know we should be responsible; it's our calling, our job, and yet we neglect, forget, leave out, do poorly. It's not that we are called to be perfect; it is, however, with this holy task that we're called to do, sometimes we don't do a very good job. It must be disappointing to God to realize that we have been called, asked and persuaded and then have not always done a good job. Certainly, God is a God of grace who forgives us and gives us another chance and yet we need to remember there are some clear responsibilities that are ours.

Our Responsibility

The call of the Great Commission in Matthew 28:18–20 reads, *"Jesus came to them and said, 'All authority in heaven and on earth has been given to me. Therefore go and make disciples of all nations, baptizing them in the name of the Father and of the Son and of the Holy Spirit, and teaching them to obey everything I have commanded you.' "* This is a call for us to act with responsibility.

The call of the judgment day story (Matthew 25:31–46) is a clear call for us to act! It reads,

> *"When the Son of Man comes in his glory, and all the angels with him, he will sit on his throne in heavenly glory. All the nations will be gathered before him, and he will separate the people one from another as a shepherd separates the sheep from the goats. He will put the sheep on his right and the goats on his left. Then the King will say to those on his right, 'Come, you who are blessed by my Father; take your inheritance, the kingdom prepared*

for you since the creation of the world. For I was hungry and you gave me something to eat, I was thirsty and you gave me something to drink, I was a stranger and you invited me in, I needed clothes and you clothed me, I was sick and you looked after me, I was in prison and you came to visit me.' Then the righteous will answer him, 'Lord, when did we see you hungry and feed you, or thirsty and give you something to drink? When did we see you a stranger and invite you in, or needing clothes and clothe you? When did we see you sick or in prison and go to visit you?' The King will reply, 'I tell you the truth, whatever you did for one of the least of these brothers of mine, you did for me.' Then he will say to those on his left, 'Depart from me, you who are cursed, into the eternal fire prepared for the devil and his angels. For I was hungry and you gave me nothing to eat, I was thirsty and you gave me nothing to drink, I was a stranger and you did not invite me in, I needed clothes and you did not clothe me, I was sick and in prison and you did not look after me.' They also will answer, 'Lord, when did we see you hungry or thirsty or a stranger or needing clothes or sick or in prison, and did not help you?' He will reply, 'I tell you the truth, whatever you did not do for one of the least of these, you did not do for me.' Then they will go away to eternal punishment, but the righteous to eternal life."

The parable of the talents (Matthew 25:14–30) is a story of our responsibility. It includes the punch line of the story: *"Master,"* he said, *"you entrusted me with five talents. See, I have gained five more."* His master replied, *"Well done, good and faithful servant! You have been faithful with a few things; I will put you in charge of many things. Come and share your master's happiness!"* The story is a story of responsibility, of us doing what we're asked to do.

The instruction at the end of the story of the Good Samaritan (Luke 10:30–37) is instruction for us to act. It reads:

"Jesus said: 'A man was going down from Jerusalem to Jericho, when he fell into the hands of robbers. They stripped him of his clothes, beat him and went away, leaving him half dead. A priest happened to be going down the same road, and when he saw the man, he passed by on the other side. So

too, a Levite, when he came to the place and saw him, passed by on the other side. But a Samaritan, as he traveled, came where the man was; and when he saw him, he took pity on him. He went to him and bandaged his wounds, pouring on oil and wine. Then he put the man on his own donkey, took him to an inn and took care of him. The next day he took out two silver coins and gave them to the innkeeper. "Look after him," he said, "and when I return, I will reimburse you for any extra expense you may have." 'Which of these three do you think was a neighbor to the man who fell into the hands of robbers?' The expert in the law replied, 'The one who had mercy on him.' Jesus told him, "Go and do likewise.' "

The story of the Good Samaritan makes it clear: we're asked to help. That's what it is to be a follower of Jesus, to do what He said. He makes it clear; He says, "Go and do."

Christianity is behavioristic. By behavioristic, I mean that it is not just what you believe in or a commitment to what you surrender; it's how you behave. Many times, we celebrate Christianity as an experience of salvation. But, much more than that, it is an experience of God's love so clearly that our behavior is changed. Granted, Paul was clear that we are saved by our faith, but he was also clear that our salvation and faith is shown in our actions. James 2:18 and 26 read, *"But someone will say, 'You have faith; I have deeds.' Show me your faith without deeds, and I will show you my faith by what I do. . . . As the body without the spirit is dead, so faith without deeds is dead."* So consequently it is normal that we feel the responsibility to do evangelism, even the guilt about not doing evangelism.

The world has turned much more secular. In this new culture we must feel a responsibility. It is imperative that we do evangelism. What the Bible teaches about our responsibility is clear: We must make disciples of Jesus Christ. These instructions that are clear in the teachings of Jesus help us to understand that being a Christian is how you behave, what you do, the action that you take. It is an imperative that we understand that responsibility. Yet, oftentimes,

Tell

we don't understand and accept the second part of that understanding of responsibility.

Our Trust in God's Power

The second part of understanding responsibility is knowing that it is a partnership, that in the midst of all of our assuming responsibility and worrying things that will be done and done right, we need to trust that God is involved with us as a partner. We're not doing this alone. Sometimes in our approach to Christianity, we become consumed by the sense of responsibility and duty, and it creates a kind of pressure so that we become legalistic, hard-nosed and authoritarian. We begin to see God as a God that demands. The teachings of Jesus teach us that God is also a God that forgives, helps and loves. The Sermon on the Mount is filled with teachings of responsibility but also teachings of God's help. We need to trust that after we do our best that God will create the growth, the new possibilities. The story of the parable of the sower (Matt.13:1–23) and the use of seed and growth throughout Christ's preaching remind us that even though we plant the seed, cultivate the soil and chase away the birds, it is God who causes the growth. There is a unique partnership that has been established in God's design for the Kingdom. We do a portion and the power of the Holy Spirit does the rest. It is a wonderful partnership. Any conversation about witnessing, sharing and telling must include our trust that God will take our efforts and produce fruitful results.

Jon and Pam had worked for years to try to help their friends Ed and Louise understand about Jesus and follow Christ. Ed had grown up in an abusive family and Louise had never attended church in her life. Her parents were agnostics, maybe atheists. They were vocal about it and made fun of the church, and ridiculed any of their children who showed any signs of faith or spirituality. So Jon and Pam tried to share the faith, tell their story and explain, but it was hard. To describe it as work was a good analogy for it was difficult. After four years of telling and inviting, Jon and Pam had invited their friends to dinner after church on Easter Sunday, thinking they would at least go to church for Easter services. Their friends made some kind of lame excuse and declined. Jon and Pam were really discouraged and, in their next Bible study group, they shared what had happened. Everyone there was sympathetic, caring and understanding. Carl was one of the really quiet people in that Bible study. He usually didn't have much to say and if he did say something it often was something brief and to the point. The group paused in the discussion when Carl spoke. What he said was simple: "Sometimes we need to trust." Someone quickly responded, "Trust what?" Then Carl with the profoundness of a great theologian said, "Trust in God!" There are lyrics of a children's song that reiterates this: "After you have done your best, your very, very best, Jesus will do the rest." Somehow in all of our strategizing and planning, in all of our meetings of leading, influencing and encouraging, we forget to trust that God will do the rest.

There is nothing that a farmer can do to get the seed to germinate. Water, sunlight and fertilizer are important, but it is up to God to get the seed to germinate and grow. So it is in evangelism. It is a partnership. After we have done our best, our very, very best, Jesus will do the rest. If we rely on and trust that partnership, we can continue to witness with enthusiasm and a sense of inner peace. One of the difficult aspects of growing in the faith is learning how to trust in God. Jesus encouraged us to take responsibility and do as He instructed, so it is imperative as a Christian that we respond to the call and do what Jesus told us to do. Yet, so often we forget or do not understand the partnership we have with God. The design of creation is one in which God is the creator, we are the followers, and God brings the growth, results and victory.

Trusting in God sometimes seems so difficult for active, energetic Christians. We read in the Sermon on the Mount in

Matthew 5–7 all of the descriptions of how we are called to be responsible. The sermon ends in Matthew 7:24–25 with an admonition that it is by building our house upon the rock of our loyalty and deeds. In Mark's gospel Jesus clearly states, *"If any want to become my followers, let them deny themselves and take up their cross and follow me"* (Mark 8:34). Too often we become convinced that we must do it all, and if someone does not accept Jesus Christ, is it our fault. We start to believe if the witness we make is not fruitful then we have made a mistake, failed our Lord or didn't do what we were told. Certainly there are times when that may be true, yet we must learn to trust in God. The Psalmist tells us simply, *"But I trust in you, O Lord; I say, 'You are my God'"* (Psalm 31:14). Simply trust God and allow Him to bring the results. This is the ultimate and most important part of evangelism. Of all the teachings about responsibility that Jesus gives, there are also continuous teachings of His love, forgiveness and grace. It is important that we understand both the trust and the responsibility.

Questions for Discussion and Personal Reflection

1. Take a few moments and write a prayer about reaching people for Christ and trusting God to bring the results.
2. Read through Psalm 31 and rewrite it simply emphasizing the aspects of trust.
3. Make a list of those people you would like to lead to Christ and then pray for them, trusting in God for results.
4. Devise ways to exercise trust: Sit in the beauty of the morning and pray. Watch the galaxies and stars at night and pray in that vastness. Hold a child in your arms and pray. Come up with your own exercises of trust.

Chapter 13
The Church Tells an Offensive Strategy

Years ago Richard Avery and Donald Marsh wrote a song titled *I Am the Church*. The words are simple: "I am the church, you are the church, we are the church together..." So often in our evangelistic enthusiasm, we see witnessing or telling the story as an individual task. We often think sharing the Gospel is something we do personally as part of our discipleship and commitment. Yet for evangelism to be effective it must be a part of the church's work. It is imperative for a committed Christian to share his faith with his friends. We are called to share our faith, and it must be part of our task of being in the church. Winning someone to Christ is not being a spiritual "Lone Ranger;" it is the job of the whole family of God working together as a community. Your personal witnessing must invite others not only to Christ but to the Church of Jesus Christ. Leading someone to Christ must involve ministry, discipleship and mission that only the church can provide. The great tragedy of the whole evangelical movement is that saved souls were considered like beads added to a necklace string. We treated people we won for Christ like good marks on our report card, without ever really caring about their discipleship or growth or what their conversion to Christ means to the Kingdom of God.

In First Corinthians 12, Paul describes the Church like a body. He says in 12:12, *"The body is a unit, though it is made up of many parts; and though all its parts are many, they form one body. So it is with Christ."* He goes on to describe us as a body, each of us having a part. The parts are different; the parts have different functions, but they are all vital parts of the whole. This is important in sharing the faith, living the faith and being a disciple—we do it as a team. Bishop Jones makes it so simple, "Faith-sharing is best done with a congregation because its goal is to initiate the non-Christian into discipleship in a congregation" (Jones, p. 75).

Each aspect of telling the story is done in cooperation with other Christians and as part of the work of the church. In this book, we have used the word "TELL" to describe what it is to share or witness to our faith. The four letters in "TELL" are a reminder of four concepts or functions of witnessing: truth, explaining, living and leading. Therefore the church must represent these four functions of witnessing in its organizational life. Evangelism is both individual and corporate. We must remember that, in order for it to be valid, it must be corporate. When the early Christians became followers of Jesus they did it to become a part of a group, the church, the community of faith and the fellowship of believers. As a group they functioned together, supported each other, sought to proclaim the good news, did acts of social justice and developed fully devoted followers of Jesus.

Too often we focus so much attention on personal witnessing that we forget that most personal witnessing does not work in the long-term unless it is done in the context of a group or the church. Even where it is effective and an act of personal witnessing leads a person to Christ, that person must become associated with a church in order to develop their faith. Most of the time when an individual becomes out of touch with the church, they lose their way and their commitment. Paul describes the church as the body of Christ in First Corinthians 12. We are individually members of a larger body. Too many times evangelistic Christians do not understand or follow this instruction from the Gospel.

Cynthia was at a church Halloween party with her daughter. She had been divorced for two years and was having a tough time. She went to the church because a friend said, "It's a good party! They're giving away lots of candy." As she watched her child play the games, she saw an old friend. Alice and Cynthia had gone to high school together but hadn't seen each other in years. They began to talk and catch up on old things and find out about each other. In the course of this, a friendship that had meant so much in high school became alive again and Cynthia shared her hurt and her anger about the divorce and Alice listened and cared. As they finished, she said, "I'm so glad you came to the party tonight! This is my church." Cynthia was surprised; Alice had not seemed very religious when she had known her growing up, but Alice seemed so caring and compassionate that evening. Cynthia wanted what Alice had. At that point, Alice could have simply shared her story and let Cynthia and her daughter go on back home to figure it out alone. But Alice understood that this task of nurturing and helping was not just a task of a conversation at a Halloween party but a long process so she invited her friend to come to church Sunday morning and attend the new singles fellowship. She also invited Cynthia's daughter to come and be a part of a Sunday school class. Both responded positively to the invitation, and, in the next weeks and months, Cynthia experienced God's love not only in conversation with her friend, Alice, but in the life and work of the church so that she became a new follower of Christ. This happened not just because of an important conversation at a Halloween party at a church but because of its church, the members and the love and the acceptance of that church.

People come to Christ in the context of the loving spirit of the church. New converts to Christianity are counted as members of the church and should be involved in doing ministry and leading other new people to Christ. It is a heresy when we turn evangelism into recruitment for our holy tally sheet on the great evangelistic scoreboard in the sky. Our victory is seen not just in the names of the people we have led to Christ, but in strengthening the church, building the kingdom of God and the conversion of the world. Therefore our witnessing and sharing of the faith are not done alone; they should always be done with the support of a community, a church. Again, Christians are not "Lone Rangers;" they are members of families and teams and work best with the support structure of a group. This book on individual witnessing is meaningless without these chapters on the church's role in leading people to Christ.

The Church Tells the Truth

Using the letters of "TELL" we are reminded that these four aspects of witnessing are always done in the context of the church. Paul said *"Now you are the body of Christ and individually members of it"* (1 Cor. 12:27 ESV). He describes the church as each of us having a task, a function in the body. So it is in witnessing. Together we witness and share the faith. Truth should always be part of the life of the church. In the midst of our frailty and the mistakes that institutions make, churches need to do their best to show Christ in church behavior and life.

The truth of most churches is the story of men and women struggling with the realities of life and overcoming the difficulties through the power of God. So the story of every church is a reflection of the story of the individual members.

A small rural church celebrates its 100th anniversary or 200th anniversary and someone begins to tell stories of how the church was started. It was farmers, ranchers or merchants who decided a church was important and necessary in the midst of pioneering American. So they sacrificed and were empowered by the Spirit of God to overcome difficulties and establish this church. It matters not where the church is in the nation or what the details of the story are, it is the story of God's empowerment. It is in that context that we share the Gospel with others. The church is a living example of the body of Christ; it is the living example of the power of Christ. Empowerment of the Hoy Spirit on the Day of Pentecost is told in the first and second chapters in the book of Acts. This is our story, because it is the story of how God works with ordinary people to create extraordinary things.

In a sense, by using advertising concepts, a church's story becomes its brand, what it is known for, what it does. It is a story of God working in the life of the people, creating a community of faith to transform the world. A medical description of the same phenomena is sometimes described as our DNA. Each individual has their own story, their DNA, or the way in which their chromosomes are put together and can be used to identify who it is. So it is at each local church. It is the story of how God has worked with them. That story becomes our beginning place and our identity.

The Church Explains the Truth

Explain becomes not only an E word in the word TELL, but a function in the church. It is education and discipleship ministries. Most sermons that are preached in the proclamation of the Gospel include an explanation of the church and of the faith. Today the task of explaining is not only the task of sermons and church educational programs but of new programs to train church members to become lay theologians who are systematic in their interpretation of faith and can answer the tough questions of life as they share their faith.

It is so important that the church today adequately teach its members to be good explainers of the faith, to understand the great doctrines, to be able to tell the message of the Scripture well, what it is they believe in and what they're opposed to. The church needs to be the school of truth, a theological school to prepare its members to lead people to Christ by sharing the explanations that are so desperately needed in a skeptical world.

The Church Lives the Truth

L has been used in this book to remind us of living the faith. If a church does not live the faith, it is hypocritical and succumbs to the criticism of a secular culture. Too often our institutional formats become our worst enemies. Instead of empowering the church to do God's work, our institutions become so bureaucratically outdated and irrelevant that they hold the living church back. Too often decisions of the bureaucrats who lead the church are decisions that have to do with territory, power and control rather than leading people to Christ. It is time for the church to begin to exemplify the priority of sharing the Gospel. Budgets, programs and other church emphases need to stop focusing on self-preservation and return to proclaiming the Gospel.

The Church Leads

The last L in the word TELL reminds us of leadership. Churches have become cultural icons hiding themselves back in the shadows and niches; they are pictures of the past and museums of what once was great in the local community. The new churches look modern and different, and thus create a new image of leadership. We are called to be churches that feed the hungry, care for the children, change the culture, stand against immorality, give people hope, minister to the hurting and lead the leaders. We need churches that are economically, institutionally and organizationally strong. For too long we have dumbed down our church life. We are no longer smart in what we do. Too often we use a defensive strategy rather than an offensive strategy.

Offensive

The search team for a new high school football coach was interviewing various candidates. After the interviews were over the school principal who led the search team said the following about one coach: "He is an offensive coach. It is time in our community and in our school that we went on the offensive. Our town needs hope, optimism, activity and enthusiasm. We need this offensive coach." Maybe that should be the description of leadership in the church today. We need leaders who are hopeful, optimistic, active and enthusiastic rather than leaders that continually try to preserve the past, to preserve the old ways. Our slogan needs to be,

"Whatever will work," rather than, "We have never done it that way." Today the church must essentially be the model, the training ground, the planning team and the victory celebration for winning people to Christ.

Today's growing churches are obviously evangelical. They are leading people to Christ. We need to be churches on the offensive. Instead of using our energy to preserve the status quo, we should learn to be creative, innovative and experiment with new methods and strategies. The first churches described in Acts 2 took risks, stood up for their beliefs and were obviously aggressive in telling the story of Christ. Today the church must TELL.

There are many types, sizes and labels that are on churches today. Some churches are more liturgical; some are less. Some are large; some are small. Some are rural; some are urban. Some churches have budgets and facilities to do magnificent things; some churches meet in one room, a house church or a small rural structure with less than 20 people. The size, finances and the setting don't matter. The call upon a local church to share the Gospel of Jesus Christ is the same in any setting. Because of the glitz and glamour of some of our larger churches, it is easy for small churches or even medium-size churches to develop a kind of church inferiority complex: We can't do it; we never can; we're going to die. It's easy to begin to give up, saying we don't have the resources or facilities and yet, with God's help, every church of every size can lead people to Christ. It seems ironic that when we're in a time of great popularity of megachurches, there's also a new popularity of house churches. House churches may be only 15 or 20 people gathered together to do God's work meeting in someone's home. Both forms can be effective in making disciples. The small form, as a new organization meeting in a house, seems unusual and progressive, while the same size church meeting in a rural area feels defeated and out of touch. Each setting has a possibility to lead people to Christ; each is called to lead people to Christ.

155

Tell

I was asked to speak in a particular part of the country where the church simply wasn't very strong. I asked the district superintendent what was the size of most of his churches. He answered most quickly, "Nearly all of them have less than 25 average attendance on Sunday morning." My first reflection was one of panic; what do I say about evangelism to a small rural church like that? I called up a friend who was the superintendent over a district much like this and I asked him to coach me, help me to know how I begin to teach evangelism to all of these very small churches. His advice was simple: "self-esteem." They need to believe that they can do it. It is time for us to listen to the power of God's Spirit in our lives. If we're a small church with only a few members, most of them belonging to the same family or two, it doesn't mean that we can't reach new people. We just have to devise the means and the method to do it. God will give us the way. It matters not whether we're large or small; the call for all of us is the same.

John Southwick, who is a part of Office of Research for the General Board of Global Ministries of the United Methodist Church, in writing in an issue of Background Data for Mission, stated, "The religious landscape of the US is changing with more people being less interested in church as we now live it out. As a result, existing and new churches are finding it more difficult to connect with the shrinking portion of the population still included, or likely to be inclined, toward church. Current modalities of congregational development are showing diminishing results in many parts of the country." John's suggestion shows a new understanding of ministry of the church that is innovative and looks positively and aggressively at the task of reaching new people for Christ. In this same article on the general topic of reaching people who are not attending church today, he states, "We must first acknowledge that getting them to come to church as usual and to plug into something there is unlikely for most. Ministry will need to go where they are and assume forms that bypass their filters against the conventional church. It may need to happen without involving a building and programs. It will need to develop relationships established in their culture and built on trust." We are called to TELL; the church is called to be evangelistic, to reach new people for Christ. The purpose of the ideas shared in this book is to call us to a new sense of optimistic, positive, hopeful, loving and aggressive understanding of the task of reaching new people for Christ. Too long, we have taken the strategy of being defensive; it's time now that we become offensive players in this game of being God's Church, God's family. We need to understand the imperative of telling the world about Jesus Christ.

Questions for Discussion and Personal Reflection

1. Read Acts 1 & 2. Summarize what happened in less than a minute.
2. List some ways your church tells the community about Jesus.
3. From your list in question 2, what is the most effective way your church actively leads people to follow Christ, become disciples and become involved in the church?
4. Is your church offensive or defensive?
5. List some ways the church still needs to be defensive in our contemporary society.
6. List some ways the church should be offensive in today's culture.
7. List an example of where you have seen the church be offensive or aggressive in telling others about Jesus in a loving way that really works.
8. List some big, effective churches today and analyze the characteristics of those churches. What are they doing that is so effective?
9. Talk about an offensive growth strategy for your church.

Chapter 14
The Church Is Truth

There are the stories about churches in most communities. In many ways churches are known because of those stories. Two old timers describe a church by saying, "Oh, that is where they had the big fire that nearly burned down the whole town," or "That is the church where the new football coach goes. He teaches Sunday school there," or "That church does lots of things for children. They are always having some kind of program for kids." Churches are known for their social action, their involvement in community projects, the status of their members and leaders, particular beliefs, unusual practices or unusual buildings. We tell stories about our churches to identify them in the community just like we tell stories about high school football teams, local merchants or a particular family restaurant. They are "identity" stories.

Too often the stories about our churches describe the worst of our behavior or at least the non-Christ like aspect of our church. We are known by unusual things that have happened at our church, community church failures or outspoken leaders. When Luke described the first church in Jerusalem he said, *"They devoted themselves to the apostles' teaching and to the fellowship, to the breaking of bread and the prayer"* (Acts 2:42). If we are to be evangelistic, make disciples of Jesus Christ, and transform the world, we need to be known clearly for that purpose. Our stories are the way people describe who we are and what we do. Our stories are sometimes a shortcut to express the secular culture's negative view of who we are. Too often our identity stories do not encourage people to follow Jesus.

Bill and Charlie had coffee at the same restaurant almost every morning after they retired. They had been friends all their lives and now that friendship had become a precious ritual. They would sit at the coffee shop, frequently joined by acquaintances, old friends, new friends or even a few enemies. The conversations were about everybody in their town. Nobody was immune and the stories that were told were partly true, partly exaggerated, but usually with a spin and a little edge. They loved to laugh at another person's troubles and repeat their failures. Their comments about the local churches could give a newcomer to the small town a pretty good picture of what the non-church community thought of each one of the churches. You could hear their quick summary about those "holy rollers," the "silk stocking" church or the church where the pastor had an affair with the secretary. Most of their stories about the local churches were not complimentary.

These two guys had long been a secular part of the community. For most of their lives they had thought they were in a distinctive minority of non-Christians. These days that doesn't seem to be so true, even in small rural American towns. In the bars, coffee shops, at the plant or outside the post office, conversations are too often about how ineffective, unkind, hard headed, close minded, arrogant and self-righteous the churches are. In the new generation younger people rarely even talk about the churches. They may simply use a word or two to summarize their feelings and move on: hypocrites, do-gooders, mean, fake, self righteous are just a few of the words they use to label most of the churches.

What Is the Truth About Church?

If the church is going to be a place where people are led to Jesus Christ, the church must be the example of Christ. Christ should be shown in the way the church members live and act in the community. The days of cultural community are gone. The post-modern era in which we live is filled with criticism for the hypocrisy of the church. If we are to win the younger generation for Jesus Christ it must be done with the integrity of being a church known as a loving organization, a caring group of people. We must be known as people who really take Jesus Christ seriously. We must minimize those acts of hypocrisy and emphasize our acts of authentically seeking to help the community.

It is time the church realizes that we no longer have a free ticket to do whatever we please in the community and be forgiven because we are the church. Being the church today means we will be criticized, made fun of, ridiculed and blamed. We are in a new day of building, a new image, a new witness to what we are and what we stand for.

Evangelism works when it is done in the context of a loving, accepting and caring community of Christians who have found the power of God's Holy Spirit in their life so vividly that Christ is seen in what they do and say both publicly and in the privacy of their own homes. The ineffectiveness of our sharing the Gospel of Jesus Christ is because we have relied on the momentum of cultural Christianity to create an attitude of forgiveness for our lack of integrity and provided excuses for our lack of determination.

We Are the Church

To tell the story of Jesus Christ and to be a witness for the Gospel is not done as simply an individual task. Rather it is the task of the corporate body of Christ. Certainly we can share the truth in our own lives and the witness of the individual Christian telling the truth, standing up for what is right, doing the good work of Christ and sharing the vitality of salvation is effective and important, but it is too often negative because of the behavior of the corporate body of Christ. We cannot lead others to Christ alone. We must be together as a team as we seek to witness and share in the secular culture of our contemporary society. Being together in sharing the faith is not just planning corporate evangelistic programs, organizing each-one-reach-one rallies, training people on how to share the

Gospel, doing random acts of kindness to provide an opportunity to witness or a host of other individual acts of evangelism that are popular. We must have the support of the community of faith not only in organizing, training and equipping, but also in the action of the church both in what it does and what it doesn't do. Because the criticism is so intense today, much of our focus is upon what we should not do as well as what we should do.

John was speaking to his youngest daughter; she was 16, driving, dating and socially active. She had quit attending church a few years before not as an in intentional act, but she just continued to have other things to do on Sunday or at other times the youth program met. She was active with her friends and just didn't seem to be interested in the church. That night when after dinner, everyone else had left the table providing John an opportunity to ask what he wanted to ask and should have asked her much sooner. He said quietly, "Honey, I have noticed you don't seem to go to church with us very much anymore." That sentence opened a long conversation. She took a breath after telling story after story of church and summarized everything by saying, "I want to believe in Jesus, and I think what you and mom have taught me is right, but I don't think the church is right. They are hypocrites, they say things that are mean and hurtful and they really don't try to help any place in the community. They are just a bunch of pious snobs, and I don't really want to be like them." John spent the next hour both listening to her and trying to help her understand why people aren't perfect or better and why the church was okay even when he knew it wasn't. The conversation ended when other members of the family entered the room. John prayed that night for his daughter, for her friends and for a world he saw going the wrong direction. He realized as he prayed that if he really wanted to make disciples, he had to not only share the faith with his daughter and other children in a clear, articulate way, but he needed to be involved in a church that really reflected Jesus Christ, and the one he was going to now simply was far from doing that. As he was finishing his prayer he felt like God was telling him clearly some very hard things he had to do, like provide leadership for his church to make significant changes in their behavior or maybe to find another church. John realized that wasn't going to be an easy task.

The story of John and his daughter is a story of committed Christians today who desire very much to lead others to Christ, whether family members or community acquaintances, and in order to do that we must do it out of the context of the church being authentic. We as the leaders of the church must assume that responsibility to bring authenticity. The criticism of the church today is so strong, the accusations of hypocrisy and irrelevancy are so accurate that the changes the church and pastors need to make could easily be described as radical. As we observe what is happening in the church today, whether we are willing to participate in radical change or not, it is happening. There is a reformation happening in the church. Part of this reformation is clearly modeled after the teachings of Jesus and part of it is simply a worship of change. It is easy to create an advocacy for change when all we are offering is simply the same irrelevant, unchristian behavior to a different tune, different order, different pastor or different church organization. The same thing with a different name doesn't mean it is different behavior. The task of the church is to tell the truth by what it is doing, what it is, how it is interpreted and what the results are.

Certainly, witnessing must be done first and foremost out of the truth of our own experience of Jesus Christ in our life and what Christ and the power of God's Spirit has done for, with and through us. It also must be shown in the church. We witness in the way we present Christ clearly in our actions, life, worship and programs of the church.

Bill and Charlie were still sitting at the same spot in the coffee shop they usually sat in and their friends and acquaintances joined them that Monday morning for coffee and conversation, for sarcastic commentary and often unkind stories and jokes. They all were surprised because Charlie told a new story. He had gone to a particular, local church, because his 10-year-old grandson was going to read the scripture that day. He loved his grandson and he wanted to be there. What he saw that Sunday and heard changed him significantly. The sermon was about God's grace and love and it was presented without arrogance. The things the pastor spoke of were unapologetically based upon the values Christ taught. The church had many programs that showed that they really cared about the community. They had programs of helping men and women who had gone through divorce deal with that struggle; they had programs for single moms and fellowship for families that were dealing with retirement; they had a crew that worked with Habitat for Humanity building a house. They offered free counseling and therapy sessions. There wasn't any arrogance, just love. Charlie shocked his groups of friends at the coffee shop that morning when he said he was going back. His grandson had asked him and he had told him he would go back to church with him. This is how evangelism should work.

The church's identity, history and image in the community are the "truth" of the church. It is more than being friendly. The church's truth is what it believes in, stands for and certainly what it does. Churches have been caught up in their self-image created by all kinds of factors in their history, culture and economic situation. Some of our churches are known by their economic prestige; they're the church for the wealthy. Other churches are known by their music program or youth program. Some churches are known by their particular liturgical actions, being very formal or charismatic or intellectual.

Summary

Churches are known by who their leader is and particular stories that happen within the life of the church that identify it for the rest of the community. It may be the story of a crisis such as a fire, a story of great generosity and helping at a time of great need, a story of effectiveness with children or youth; churches develop their image or brand through their behavior, members and particular situations. This is natural and is the simple way which we in any culture identify groups of people. The important thing in the midst of all these choices of how we are known in the community is the truth of our experience with Jesus Christ.

One of the ways that behavior is explained is through the influence of beliefs; that is, our identity is often explained by particular behavior, historical events or place in culture. Another way to understand our identity is through our beliefs–what we are committed to, what we believe in and what we stand for. We know that those commitments, beliefs and ideals direct our behavior. So our identity then becomes a collection of both our behaviors and the beliefs that are behind them. Our commitment to Jesus Christ, then, should the truth of our church's life. Certainly, all the other things that are a part of the church's history, its existence and its cultural place in the community are important; our witness to new people and impact upon the children and youth of our community is directly related to the truth of our own beliefs, our commitments and our ideals. The T in the word "Tell" is a reminder for a local church that the truth of our own experience, life and beliefs becomes the beginning of our ability to reach new people for Christ. It also directs who we are able to reach.

A small church in a rural area made a decision to make youth the priority for the church. It was out of that priority that they began to hold certain kinds of programs, activities and ministries that met the needs of youth. Those in the community began to

identify and talk about the church that really helped families of
youth. Because of that commitment and set of beliefs the local
church was able to meet an increasing number of youth and their
families in the community.

Another church in an urban area of mostly elderly people made
a commitment to make it a priority to care for people in retirement.
They had programs, activities and ministries because they believed
that that God what was calling them to do. As a result of that decision, the church reached more older people. That's who they chose
to be, and, in the programming and life of the church, their truth
was evident. We need to know and understand that the truth of our
experiences and decisions about our identity influence how we are
able to reach people. Certainly this becomes powerful when we are
clear about Christ being the center of our beliefs, purpose and
direction.

In the camp meeting days of the past, after the summer harvest,
people would gather under what were called brush arbors for revival
meetings. The revival meetings had two purposes: one was to
strengthen the commitment of the church; the second was to reach
new people. Fulfilling both of these purposes was a priority. In the
years that followed that period of history, the concept of a revival
became the mark of a healthy church: reviving the Spirit of Christ
and the purpose and dedication to Christ became an understood
necessity for every local church in order to be clear on its mission
and purpose to make disciples of Jesus Christ. Our culture has
changed; we no longer have revival meetings. We're no longer a
rural community where we gather under brush arbors and recom-
mit, but the need for keeping clear about the truth of who we are is
absolute. We must be clear about our decision to be a church following Jesus Christ.

The members of the administrative board were frustrated that
evening when the pastor explained that the denominational

executives had asked every local church to write a three-sentence mission statement that would explain what the church is and what its truth is. The board argued; some said it was unnecessary; some said it was impossible; some had a pet doctrine, program or idea that they hoped would be in the first sentence of mission statement. The task of being clear about our experience of God's power in our life as a local church is a crucial question for us in being able to evangelize to others. Too often, we evangelize by being the friendly church or the music church or the children's church or. . .the list goes on. It's time for us to be clear about what we believe and what we stand for.

Questions for Discussion and Personal Reflection

1. What are some things the Church needs to change to be more like Christ?
2. What are some of the things your church needs to change to be more like Christ?
3. Why are Christians called hypocrites?
4. Discuss what the church should do to be clearly understood as an example of Jesus Christ's teachings. Make a list of the characteristics of that kind of church.
5. What does your church need to be a Christ-like church?
6. Discuss what you would need to do to be a part of the leadership and create this kind of a church, a church truly reflective of Christ. What do you need to do in your church?
7. Spend some time in prayer for the church, for your local church, for the churches in your community and the churches in the world.

Chapter 15
The Church Explains

A well known, successful pastor often chooses the sermon series following Easter or Christmas to be a series that deals with controversial, problematic and difficult topics. He believes that Christmas and Easter are the build-up and what happens after are the results. It is in those Sundays following the sweetness of Christmas and Easter that the hard issues of faith need to be discussed. Because we have become a society of question askers, we want to know: why does it work that way, how does this work, what is the motivation, what is the real meaning behind it or what is the story behind the story? We have become skeptical and we want to know.

The Church: A School of Theology

Christians can no longer be afraid to tell the truth and to explain. We need to explain about God what we know and what we don't know, explain what the idea of the Trinity is all about and what it seeks to describe and explain what Jesus really taught, what He said. We need to explain what the church practices are and why the church does certain kinds of things. We need to explain the history of the church and what the gift of freedom has meant in terms of diversity. The fact that the church is not agreed on everything is not a sign of weakness but is a celebration of the freedom that God has given the church. The church should be a school of apologetics.

They had been nominal Christians. They went to church from time to time. This couple probably went to church because their friends did and it was good business. They had a successful department store in a medium-sized town. For good business they needed to belong to a church. But it was only after their children had grown, as they were empty nesters and after he battled cancer that they really rethought their faith and committed their lives to Christ. Their lives changed dramatically. They were different. Their 27-year-old son had a hard time with these changes. Finally, he said to his dad, "Dad, I don't understand. All those years you took me to church, maybe once every three months. It didn't seem to matter at all. You seemed like you were more interested in successful business than successful living. Now you have changed. You are moral, you have integrity and you are such a loving man. I don't understand how going to church and you making a commitment to Christ finally made you so different." Then he paused for a moment and said, "Dad, I am a scientist. I have been one since I was a boy. I need a simple answer. I want to know what following Jesus Christ really means to you. How has it changed your life? What is it that you really believe in and why do you believe in it today?" Then he spoke as sincerely as he ever spoke to his father. He said, "Dad, I want what you have, but I don't want 'pat' answers. I want real explanations." He kind of laughed and said, "Dad, I want you to be a theologian and explain it."

The Church Must Train Lay Theologians

What most secular people need today is for Christians to be good theologians and explain our beliefs and practices. This means that the local church needs to take the whole matter of lay theological education more serious than we have done before. We need to train our members to be good Bible students. They need to know not just enough to get by, but enough to explain to the most skeptical 27-year-old. We need to train our committed Christians to be systematic theologians so their explanations make sense. They need to share explanations not built upon the emotion of the moment but upon the logic of the ideas. We need to learn what the great theologians have taught and learn how to explain it in a simple way. The church needs to be a school of theology as well as a place of peace, joy and service. We need to not be afraid of any controversial subject and recognize we will make mistakes and not always have it right. For the church to really be a part of witnessing in the twenty-first century the church must be a systematic school of Bible and theology. The church should be a place to learn the answers, a school of apologetics.

The church must teach the answers and expect our members to learn and study how to explain. Witnessing today is based on the individual Christian's experiences, emotion and personal struggle. It must be "reality Christianity" to be meaningful to the secular person. It also must be logical, systematic and mature and "make sense." The non-Christian wants to know and understand as well as feel authentic and at peace.

One of the most important ways that the church can help the individual Christian be an explainer is by intentionally teaching the full aspects of being a Christian disciple. We must help the Christian disciple know how to explain the great doctrines in a practical way and to understand the sophistications of a Christian faith. We must help the Christian know ways to explain which respect the learner and are practical in their application and clear in their understanding.

One of the major issues for the Christian today is what does it mean to be a Christian. Simply, how do you follow Jesus? One of the great criticisms of the church is that, as Dan Kimball stated in his book of the same name, they like Jesus but not the Church. Because the Church has been unclear and not always helpful, it is important that we spend time teaching what Jesus taught. Jesus gave us the great commandments: "Love God and love your neighbor as yourself" (Luke 10). We need to be prepared to explain these rules and challenge people to follow. In Romans 13, Paul says *"All the law and all the commandments can be summarized as simply love your neighbor as yourself."* We need to be prepared to explain love simply and clearly.

Tell

Christian Education

Lay schools of theology, sermons on the great doctrines of faith, adult and youth Sunday school lessons dealing with the issues of systematic theology and classes on the tough questions of the Christian faith are all ways we must provide the cognitive tools that a contemporary Christian needs today in order to explain.

In the church, much energy is used in teaching. The local church is busy teaching the children, teaching adult classes, teaching sermons and teaching Bible studies. To really become an empowering church for helping people explain the faith, we need to become a lay school of theology–a place where the lay leaders can be trained as systematic theologians to answer the tough questions being asked in our society. This training certainly is done in the traditional ways such as adult and young adult classes or children and youth classes. It is also done as a part of the Bible study program of a church. Leaders need to carefully look at their curriculum plans as they evaluate the question of how well are they preparing the laity of the church to answer the tough questions in our society.

Churches may create lay academies, spiritual formation academies, lay theological educations schools and whatever necessary is necessary to institutionalize and popularize the importance of offering quality, practical theological education. The education needs to be offered in a way that is not only for the benefit of the learner but for the benefit of the teachers themselves. We need to learn the meaning of the atonement for ourselves but also learn how to talk about the atonement in a tough conversation with an agnostic. Doctrines that have to do with baptism, Holy Communion, worship, the Trinity, the nature of God and the nature of human beings are all essential questions for a Christian to understand and be able to explain. But most importantly we need a clear understanding of what it is to follow Jesus. What did Jesus teach us? What is it to follow Him? We need to know words that explain well, metaphors that hold the truth and have practiced our explanations. The answer to why bad things happen to good people is not only an important theological question that every Christian has to find an answer to, but it is also the heart of so many discussions in our secular world. We need answers and we need training in order to use those answers well.

No More Dumb Church

Preaching is the heart of the worship service and the worship service is the heart of the Christian community. For too long we have made sermons too simple because the laity were biblically and theologically untrained Christians. Sermons need to be communicated well by pastors who know the drama of worship, the good use of metaphor, humor and story, and learning theory. We also need sermons that explain and are intellectually clear and challenging. Certainly sermons are not helpful if they are so academic they leave the congregation in an entanglement of complex ideas and concepts. However, we should not avoid the tough questions and hard theological issues in our sermons. Most pastors will find sermons that deal with those tough questions are worship services where the attendance is up rather than down. Congregations want to know answers because we are being asked the questions. In many ways the inability of the Christian to answer the hard questions is a result of avoidance of controversial issues by the church. All too often, an unwillingness to admit that we are wrong or that we don't know has hampered our ability to make new disciples. It has created a kind of dumb church. It is time we relooked at our task of a church, not to become intellectual elite but to become the power in helping people understand as well as experience the faith.

Conclusion

As we seek to reach a changing society with a multiplicity of issues and a variety of belief systems and religious points of view, it is important that Christians know clearly what they believe, what

Jesus taught and how to explain it and share it lovingly. The church has spent a great deal of time and effort in training clergy. Too often, our training of laity is superficial. It's time for us to deal with the major issues of the nature of God, the nature of the future, ethics, morality, dignity and the primary ideas that Jesus Christ taught.

Questions for Discussion and Personal Reflection

1. What are some of the tough questions that non-Christians ask the church today?
2. Pick out one or two of these tough questions and think how you might answer or explain.
3. List several ways the church should teach the explanations to the faith.
4. How do you answer the tough questions of faith? Choose one of the following and explain it in a way that a skeptic could understand:
   a. Why do bad things happen to good people?
   b. What is the doctrine of the atonement and why it so important?
   c. What do Christians believe about the importance of baptism? How is it done and why?
   d. What is the nature of human beings? Are people basically good or bad?
   e. Summarize simply what Jesus taught His followers to do.
5. What are some of the ways in which the whole task of Christian education could be done better in your church? What are some ideas and suggestions for improvements?
6. Make a plan for effective lay theological education in your church.

Chapter 16
The Church Witnesses by the Church's Life

This is sometimes a skeptical world. It is a world that criticizes Christians for being hypocrites. How the Christian lives is a very strong witness. What the church does speaks very loudly. Hypocritical actions by the church are very negative to non-Christians.

He came home from work late that night. She knew this was the afternoon that he and his buddies usually stopped on the way home for beer and she expected him to be late. When he came through the back door he slammed it with such emotion she knew something was wrong. He walked into the kitchen where she was fixing dinner for the family and he just was so angry he could hardly talk. She put her arm on his shoulder and said, "What is wrong? Tell me." He said, "I am so angry at that pastor." She said, "What do you mean? What pastor, your pastor?" He said, "No, No." He then told her he was mad at a clergy person of a church across town.

She knew immediately who the clergy was. His name had been in the newspaper over and over recently. He had had an affair with a member of the church and was found guilty of stealing money from the church. He resigned publically. The church was devastated. The newspapers were telling a part of the story over and over, day after day. It was on television and even made the national news for one day. Everybody knew. She turned to her husband and said, "What did this preacher do to you?" Then he explained to her, "I have been working with Sam for two years. He is the most skeptical agnostic I have ever known. He asks so many questions! I have patiently answered question after question. I didn't know that Sam had been visiting Rev. Jackson's church. Sam is just blown out of the water." "What do you mean?" she said. He replied, "I really thought he was coming around. He was understanding. The skepticism that was bred into him by his family, and the anti-religious feelings that were developed while he was a teenager were going away. When I heard he was going to Jackson's church I thought maybe he was really changing. Today, he is back where he was two years ago. He says he will never go to church again. He says that Jackson was a liar. I tried to explain that pastors are human and everybody makes mistakes, but it didn't work. Sam is so negative about God, Jesus and the Bible. I spent two years and now it is all wiped out by one pastor's stupid behavior." This story is not just about a pastor's unwise behavior, it is a reminder that our society today takes the missteps of Christians as a sign of the dysfunction of the faith.

The Authentic Church

Society has become so skeptical. People love to find examples of failure of those in places of leadership and when it is church leadership, it is amplified by this secular sarcastic society. The negative attitude toward Evangelical Christians spills over on all Christians, and, when one of us makes a mistake, particularly when it is public, it reflects on all of us. But more than that, it reflects on Jesus. We need to live the faith. We need to understand that children, adults and teenagers are watching. We can't be perfect; we are going to make mistakes. The stakes are high and the need for integrity, honesty, love and genuineness is so great. It is a characteristic greatly desired by contemporary society. Authenticity, honesty and integrity have become prime values. We as Christians speak about all that Christ has done for us, we need to share the faith by the way that we live.

The church must be as authentic. Churches make mistakes just like people do. Because we live in a corporate world, local churches need to show that integrity and honesty. A church that proclaims love and isn't openly willing to welcome people of different races and ethnic groups is condemned by the secularist before they have even heard our story. A church that uses money unwisely in a society that is economically in trouble is a church that adds to the skeptical attitude about the positive effect of Jesus. Local churches need to practice as much integrity in business practices and relationships as any individual Christians. Local churches need to show that they are authentic by their programs of helping other people and by being there to care. The church is there to meet our needs. It is there to show that God is available to meet our needs.

Evangelism based upon meeting needs is a way in which we show that the love of Jesus Christ is real. Churches that are self-centered, unconcerned, prejudiced, unresponsive, arrogant or close-minded destroy the authenticity of the message of the love of Jesus Christ.

The Church Witnesses by What It Does

The task of witnessing is not just an individual's task of living up to the Gospel. It is the whole church's task together. People who have made a decision to seek employment through the church either as a call or a job need to understand they have an additional responsibility. Being on the staff of the church calls for careful responsibility, morality and integrity. The sins of the pastors and other church staff and leaders in recent years are maybe the most destructive thing to the church today. The hypocrisy of church leaders tells skeptical young adults that the church is a lie. The indiscretions of pastors, staff and members need to be called into radical question by the leaders of the church.

We need to deal with our behavior as a church, whether it is child abuse, sexual inappropriateness, financial mismanagement, prejudice or any behaviors that are the opposite of what Christ taught. These must be stopped if we are to be more effective in winning people over to the power of Jesus Christ.

A downtown church in Peoria, Illinois created a partnership with the church leaders and the local community recreation program to provide coaches and support for the teams in the community recreation program. The church members became coaches for those neighborhood teams in the inner-city. One of the coaches asked a simple question at a coaches meeting, "Do you suppose our kids would like not only to play football and baseball but would like to sing in a choir?" Some of the other coaches laughed for a moment and then said, "Maybe." The team of church coaches offered the kids a choir and the kids loved it. They sang in the choir, and, as the choir sang more often at church, the kids and their parents began to come to church. The community was changed, the Gospel was shared and the church became more loving and reached more of the community.

In His Steps: A Model

The church I served in Tulsa studied Charles Sheldon's book, *In His Steps*, and decided they wanted to ask what Jesus would do. They believed what Jesus would do is what He said in Luke 10, to help people in need and be a Good Samaritan church. So they began their own survey of the needs. They went to the local high school and asked, "What are the needs?" They went to the local community action committee and asked, "What are the needs?" They asked the members of the church what their needs were. Among the needs was a need for help with families, marriage problems, drugs and vocational planning. The church decided to open a counseling center. The counseling center eventually had eight full-time staff and became a main place for help in the community and literally hundreds of people came to the church because it cared. It became a church that did what Jesus would do.

The Church Shows the God Story

Too often we think that our witnessing is an individual thing. Certainly it is often done individually. Witnessing is done also in the context of the corporate identity of the church of Jesus Christ. From the day of Pentecost until today successful evangelism has happened by groups of people telling the story of God. Certainly the stories are individual but the impact comes from the group.

Witnessing and the story are always done in the context of other followers of Jesus. Andrew brought Peter not just to see Jesus, but to become a part of the church, the followers of Jesus. So it is in the aspect of witnessing that is to tell your own story. The meaning of your story is certainly an individual meaning. The results are individual, but they are also corporate. The church today must realize that in a highly skeptical, very secular world the church needs to set positive examples of Christians witnessing to what Christ means.

This means the old-fashioned testimony meeting that once was reserved to a handful of loyal Christians on Wednesday night must become a part of what the church does on Sunday or any time the church is presenting the Gospel. It needs to be presented not only as systematic theology, and biblical relevance, but also in as personal spiritual power. Mainline churches usually have only properly qualified and trained theologians behind the pulpit. Today we realize without having the practical stories of ordinary men and women's sharing their faith, the Gospel seems remote and unreal. The personal testimony by ordinary churchmen or extraordinary members or community leaders is needed today.

In a world that relies heavily on authenticity, we want to know if it really works. Does following Jesus make a difference at the office, shop, in the coal mine and on the farm? The skeptical, post-modern thinker wants to know, does following Jesus really make a difference in the way you raise your family, in the way you build a home and a marriage? The church needs to make as a part of its major emphasis the telling of the truth of what Christianity is about, what it does for you, what the benefits are, what the power is and what the peace is. Worship services need to include testimonies and stories of individuals living out their faith.

Today in our culture there is much interest in religion and matters that are spiritual. People want to know what others believe. Statisticians and sociologists have said that interest in church has declined radically in the last 20 years while interest in spiritual matters has increased. The world wants to know what your Christianity does for you. Does it work? Does it matter? Does it change things? This means that a whole new way of talking about church needs to be a part of the way the church presents itself in the media. In an ad it places in a local newspaper, in a sign in front of the church, in the names in sermons, in the way church programming is done and in every case the story of what God means to us as individuals must be a part of that presentation. Churches can be creative in all kinds of ways to tell the story, but the story will capture the attention of the community in a way that flat, logical, theological jargon does not. The practical story will capture a skeptical young adult in a way that fear and guilt never can.

Evangelism Is the Church's Task

Evangelism should not be something that churches do when they need more contributors to pay a building debt off or something that people do once a year at Easter when they ask people to join. For evangelism to work, it must be developed around the program of a healthy and helping local church. The local church shows the power of the Gospel of Jesus Christ by the way in which it helps people in the midst of whatever their needs are, whatever the crisis may be, whatever the situation that exists in their life. Jesus' Great Commission to go make disciples of all nations is an absolute kind of instruction for the church. Certainly, the church has many ways to describe its task, but there is no way that it is clearer than the Great Commission; it is what it means, as Paul described in First Corinthians 12, the Body of Christ.

Old Ways Don't Work

There was a time when people could witness for Christ in a way that was almost arrogant, built upon guilt and fear. Because of the dominance of the Christian culture in the past, individuals felt cultural pressure to be a Christian and join the church. Back in the days of camp meetings, sinners came to the camp meetings. The front benches in the camp meeting arbor were called mourner's benches. They were where the sinners sat waiting to hear the Gospel, repent of their sins and be saved. Today that kind of personal witnessing is extremely uncommon and ineffective. Sinners don't sit on the front row "mourner's bench." People are antagonistic toward the church. Non-Christians see the church as irrelevant and hypocritical. If the witness is only a condemning statement of guilt and fear, most non-Christians today respond in an extremely negative way. They don't believe they need what the church has; they don't believe they need Jesus. They have little emotional reaction to talk of the atoning power of Jesus Christ, their guilt of sin and their need for repentance.

In First Corinthians 12 Paul called the Church the body of Christ. We are the picture of Jesus Christ today. What we do as the church is the witness.

In the past the church used invitational evangelism. Just invite them to church. Invite the non-Christians, the sinners and the secular people to church. Since everybody knows that you need to go to church everybody knows that good, successful and honorable people go to church. The invitation is all that is needed. Today, with the church's bad reputation and the criticism of hypocrisy, so often the invitation to church is an entertainment invitation. Come to church and see what we have to offer come to church and see "the really big show." Come to church and see the concert or the play. These invitational events certainly are good ideas and do get people to church, but people are not led to Christ; they are simply led to a new experience. They will come back if and when we have a new experience better than the previous one. Invitation evangelism works when the entertainment is good but it works only to get people in the room. The prospective Christian is there not because they are looking for help or seeking Christ or answers, they are at church because of the entertainment. Maybe they will hear the Gospel and be touched, but mostly they will see and hear the entertainment.

What Does Work?

For witnessing of an individual Christian to work today, it needs to be done in the context of an authentic church that is sharing an authentic Gospel and seeks to meet the real needs that exist within our society. Jesus said that He came to heal the sick. If we are to follow Jesus, we need to be there to heal the hurt, sick and suffering. The 25th chapter of Matthew ends with a judgment day story where Jesus makes it clear, *"Truly I tell you, just as you did not do it to one of the least of these, you did not do it to me. And these will go away into eternal punishment, but the righteous into eternal life"* (Matthew 25:45–46). In Luke's gospel Jesus explains love and Christian behavior clearly in the story of the Good Samaritan (Luke 10:25–37). It is a story of someone helping another person who was in need. The Church today is called to be a place of meeting needs, ministry and help and, in the meeting needs, helping and doing ministry, we share the living Christ. The Church must not offer an entertainment Christ nor a fearful Christ, but a living, loving Jesus Christ. What the Church does is the same thing that Jesus did by the well as He healed the blind, at the meeting when He healed the 10 lepers and in the crowd as He stopped the bleeding from the woman who had hemorrhaged for most of her life. When the non-Christian sees the power and help of the Gospel of Jesus Christ, then he sees Jesus. And, when he commits, he commits to the loving Jesus Christ who helps, changes and empowers, neither the entertaining Jesus nor the fearful Jesus. He commits to the loving, helping Jesus. This is the Church!

I have called the strategy of reaching people based upon their needs *Needs-Based Evangelism.* It is showing how the power of Christ helps. The best advertisement for a church is not necessarily how good the choir is but how helpful the parenting program is; it is not so much the degrees that the pastor has or number of associate pastors on the church staff as it is the number of programs that a local church has that really does help. The stories of the help and relevance of the local church tell the truth of the Gospel.

Needs-Based Evangelism is a way to talk about reaching people by helping and meeting their needs. Just as Jesus healed the sick and healed the hurts of the brokenhearted, and, with the injustices of His society, cared for the needs of poor, so we need to be responsive to where the hurts are in our society. Needs-based evangelism is built upon a concept of a church really studying the needs within their community that the particular local church can meet. It is the process of the laity of the church developing programs and ministries that really help, where the Gospel is integrated and people see Christ and become involved in the church through those ministries and eventually make a commitment to follow Christ as well as be part of His church.

Needs-Based Evangelism

The stories of this approach's effectiveness come from all across the church and from all kinds of denominations.

A local church developed a recovery ministry and, in the midst of that 12-step program, lives were changed. Alcoholics who were part of the 12-step program in the small groups of recovery shared their story and told how Jesus had brought them peace and power. Out of that caring, the participants in the recovery ministry people, came to know Christ, know the church and experience love. They made a decision to commit to Christ and, in doing so, they committed not only to Christ but to be people of ministry. It's not that they joined the church, it is that they became the church.

A neighborhood church organized a young mom's club. The young moms shared and built loving fellowship. The club was developed by committed evangelistic members of the church. Women came for fellowship and community. They found these and they found Christ, and they in turn became the church.

A church with a declining youth group decided that they must revitalize the youth program. They developed a new youth program with a focus upon helping kids and really meeting their needs as well as the needs of their families and parents. As more kids came to be part of the youth program, their parents become part of the organizational structure. New programs and better programs were developed, and as the youth group grew, the church grew. New people committed to Christ. New leaders became active in the church. The church grew with people who were helped and were really led to Christ.

The list of needs that the church today can help and support is endless. Some of those needs that have developed in Needs-Based Evangelistic planning conferences include singles ministry, single parents, widow and widower support group, parents of pre-adolescents support group, heart patients support group, exercise groups, job hunting support group, pre-retirement classes, mission teams, hospital waiting room ministries, handicapped children and parents support group, grandparents raising grandkids group and the list goes on and on. When the church is doing these ministries of care, people (the "body of Christ") come and become part of the church through the ministry. They come to know Christians and Christ. They are changed by the power of the Holy Spirit. These people begin their journey to become fully devoted followers of Christ and members of His church. They are involved and they become the organizers of new ministries to reach new people.

Live the Faith

Advocates of evangelism have devised all kinds of programs with many different slogans over the years. The simple model of helping people in need doesn't need a slogan, it just needs action. The best example of living a Christian faith is to be there to help. In Matthew 25, Jesus describes how our life is to be evaluated. We will stand there before the judgment throne and the question will be asked, "What have you done for the least of these?" We are called to be involved in the world to help. The church that meets the needs of the community is a church that will be growing.

Trevor was an active member of his local church and had been for some time. Most people didn't realize that Trevor was an alcoholic; he had been before he came to the church, and he still was. He was deeply involved in the 12-step program; he regularly attended meetings and had been sober for 12 years. When he heard about another church in another city doing a recovery program he went, learned about it and visited the church. Afterwards, he came back to his home church and did everything he could to convince his church that they needed to start what has been called "Recovery" program. In developing this ministry he led new people to Christ and increased the vitality and activity of the church, and met the needs of many people in the community.

Needs-Based Evangelism is an evangelism method that focuses where the hurts are and where the needs are. Jesus spoke of His ministry as one that was for those who hurt and those who are sick. This is the church's ministry today. In doing this, we live the faith.

One busy Sunday, an older member of my congregation came to me and asked if the church could help her as a grandparent raising her grandchildren. She spoke about how great the need was and how she had talked with three other grandparents in the church about how our church should start that ministry. We did. The lives of both grandparents and their grandchildren were changed. A need that no one was paying any attention to was met in a beautiful, loving Christian way. The grandparents support group and the grandkids' involvement in the church became an example of Christ's love. A new Sunday school class was started and the grandparents eventually became active as part of the youth sponsor team. Out of this ministry, people accepted Christ including children, youth and adults. Out of this ministry the church grew significantly.

One of the grandfathers caught me in the hallway one Sunday and said, "You know, I had given up on the church. I went to church as a kid but I haven't been to church since then. My wife dragged me along to this grandparents deal since we are taking care of our grandkids now. I have never seen such love and concern as I have from this church." A tear formed in the corner of his eye and he choked as he said, "My life has changed because of what I have seen you people do. I am a Christian. I never thought I wanted to be one. I am one now!" Today the strongest witness is to live the faith. The Church must meet the needs as Jesus commanded us to do.

Needs-Based Evangelism Leads People to Christ

Jesus described His ministry in Luke 4 in terms of meeting the needs of people. If we are to follow Christ, we must be willing to meet the needs of people whatever their circumstance might be. The beautiful thing about being a church that meets needs is that people come to the church not because of entertainment or even an attractive invitation, but because they receive God's help and their needs are met. In this secular world, we realize very clearly that it isn't necessarily popular to go to church; certainly it is for some, but for secular people the resistance is strong. When a person is hurting, has gone through a divorce, is battling cancer or is dealing with parenting problems, then people are more open to answers, even from the church. To be like Christ is to be there to help people who are in need. It is out of that need people come to know who Christ is. The old ways of building attendance was through invitation and hospitality alone, hoping we catch someone and get them into church. Needs-Based Evangelism means helping a person in the midst of their need to realize that Christ is the answer and provides the opportunity for the individual to be at church not by intimidation or even hospitality, but because the church is where there is help.

Needs-Based Evangelism is Christ- and church-centered. The cancer support group includes prayer and an invitation to attend Sunday school next Sunday morning. The parenting classes are incorporated into the youth program, so the youth in the parenting class are invited to go to the youth activities that same evening. The grandparents support group is an outward ministry of one of the older persons' Sunday school classes. By doing and living like Christ taught, we show Christ. It is in this action that Christ becomes present and people are lead to know Him and follow Him.

Questions for Discussion and Personal Reflection

1. What are some of the serious mistakes or faults of the church that block people from following Jesus?
2. Often Christians are described as hypocritical. What does the church do that makes Christians seem hypocritical? Make a list.
3. If your church simply taught and did what Jesus taught, what would the impact be upon the community?
4. How can local church programs of meeting the needs and helping people be an effective way of sharing the Gospel?
5. What does your church do to meet the needs of people within the community?
6. If you were going to be part of the best possible example of a church following Jesus, list four things that your church would do.

Chapter 17
The Church Leads

The story of faith found in the Bible is filled with examples of leadership. Moses was called by God to lead the Hebrew people out of captivity. He led them out of slavery, through the sea, through the wilderness and to the Promised Land. The story of David is God calling the Hebrew nation into strength and the struggle of that leadership. The book of Acts is a story of the leadership of the Church, the Church's establishment of itself, its ethics, morality and sense of purpose in life through the stories of leaders such as Paul, Peter, James, Luke and John. The church is often seen as a fortress, refuge and hiding place. At times we need that function of the Church, but the Church is called most often and most clearly in its biblical story to be a leader. The Church is called to be a leader in culture, a leader of people, a leader through times of difficulty and a leader to create a better world. The concept of kingdom is a concept of our calling as a Church. The Lord's Prayer focuses on our goal: *"Your kingdom come, your will be done"* (Matthew 6:10).

Divine Imperative

As the individual feels the imperative to share the Gospel. It is, as Emil Bunner called it, a "divine imperative." This imperative calls us to reenact the day of Pentecost every day and lead people to become followers of Jesus Christ. This is God's orders, direction and instruction. We are told we must lead others to faith. We must as Christians follow the "imperative." We must understand this is a task done by individuals working together as a group following God's instructions. The story of the day of Pentecost is a story of particular individuals and also a story of a group. As the Body of Christ we are working together each in our way and each in our own function to accomplish the goals of the Kingdom. Too often evangelism is seen as a "Lone Ranger" activity. An individual who shares the faith may invite the person and lead them to accepting Christ then never follows up or helps the new Christian grow. That is not effective evangelism. Evangelism is a function of a group of people loving, caring, supporting, ministering and asking others to join them in the crusade to change society. The slogan oftentimes used, "Each one Reach one" is only half valid. For if it is only the task of each one reaching one, evangelism would be nothing more than some kind of hunting expedition for the saint who gets a reward for saving a sinner. The work of leading people to Christ is something we should do together. People are led to Christ not individually, but in the context of the local church.

The classic story of a devout Christian meeting an individual in the marketplace or in the workplace and sharing their faith in such a dramatic way that the individual is convinced and accepts Jesus Christ most often doesn't end in satisfaction, but ends in failure. A person grows in the faith because they are in the church, the Christian community. It's more than going to a church; you must be involved in a church. We are doing this task together. The love of God that happens in conversion happens through people. Therefore, for us to be able to lead people to Christ, we need the support of our church and friends, and we need to work together as a team. The task of making a disciple is a task of a whole community of people sharing, learning and leading. The church leads people in its life, teachings, service and worship.

Keith really had never gone to church. He had gone a couple of times as a kid with friends and his grandmother had taken him to her church when he had visited her. But he really never understood it. He was skeptical, sometimes angry at the church and, most of the time, he just ignored it. It wasn't a part of his life until some things began to happen.

The doctor said Keith had cancer and the treatments would be extensive. He was devastated. Cancer wasn't in his family health history and wasn't in his plan. At 54 years of age, he was afraid he was dying. That Sunday morning he was surfing the channels while his wife sat in the living room reading the Sunday paper. The television landed on a worship service and the pastor was talking about God's love. The pastor was articulate and clear. He felt affirmed by the pastor speaking at University of Tulsa. He was told of how God loves us, helps us and heals us. Keith for the first time heard the old story. When the 30-minute broadcast was over, he sat in his lounge and bawled. His wife heard the sounds and came into the family room where the television was. She didn't know what to do. She couldn't understand what had happened. It was so unlike him, but she knew it had to have something to do with the cancer. She touched him and held him. Although she didn't know why he was crying she cried too. Then he told her. He told her that he had accepted Jesus Christ as his Lord and Savior. She was overwhelmed, bewildered, frustrated and sympathetic all at the same time. She understood why and what was going on and yet she didn't really understand. They talked about it most of the rest of the day. They called a friend that they knew went to church. They needed to understand what was happening and what it was all about. Their friend, by the grace of God, was wise and loving. She came over that afternoon and they talked. Two days later he had a meeting with his friend's pastor and they talked. Yet, as sincere as Keith was he still felt empty. They talked to him about baptism and made plans for his baptism and yet somehow it just didn't fit together. It did fit together at the same church in the cancer support group. The first Sunday Keith attended, he saw an announcement about it in the bulletin and commented to his wife after church that he would like to visit. He found out when they met, and he showed up. It would take many pages to describe what happened, but it was in the cancer support group that Keith came to know Jesus Christ. It was in the love that was shared by those Christian men and women that he came to know about the love of God. It was in the stories that they told that he came to understand the meaning of the Spirit of God being with us. It was in the testimonies of the men and women who told how their lives were changed; that Keith came to know what Jesus Christ really taught. The church activates, organizes and carries out the process of leading someone to Christ.

Leading someone to Christ is a process of a group; it is the work of the church. Unless the church is willing to organize itself to lead people to Christ, real evangelism will not happen. People may say the magic words of confession, but they will never become disciples. That is why the Church was created—to do the work of Christ. It is the body of Christ.

The church leads by its program, fellowship and life!

The Invitational Church

As a church seeks to support its members in being evangelistic and, at the same time, be the center of teaching, learning and discipleship, it must be invitational. It needs to be a place you want to go, full of people you want to be around, an experience that is valid and authentic. It should be positive and attractive. Whether through the décor, the worship service or the hospitality of the congregation, church should be invitational. This is why church life needs to be Christ like. Church life must be authentic, loving, caring and just. What we do in our organizational life needs to be a true reflection of Christ's truth and power. The church needs to be a witness in its leadership; therefore it needs to plan its program so they reach out. The programs need to be indicative of Needs-Based Evangelism, developed on the basis of the needs and hurts of the community. Worship needs to be invitational so that personal witnessing is supported by worship that truly is authentic and draws people to it. Our worship so often is boring, out of touch, irrelevant and sometimes even embarrassing. We need to do worship that draws people to it, that answers their questions and tells the stories. Worship needs to involve ordinary laity and their stories as well as pastors explaining the faith.

Church leadership must do more than just invite; they must organize ways to show the love of God through relationship and through fellowship. Hospitality ministries are often mentioned as a part of evangelism, and, indeed, they are the way the church proves that it is a part of the body of Christ. Through hospitality, the church members share the love. Whether it is a nametag board, a greeter at the door, a welcoming song or the worship of a church it should be invitational, welcoming and full of love. Too often the design of church is stuck in the rut of the way things have always done. Although that is comfortable and satisfying to many of the members, our task is to reach new people for Christ and many of those new people care nothing about the tradition. New people are interested more in the content.

Church Leadership in Worship

We need to do worship in a way that communicates. Sometimes that is a new way. For instance, since a majority of human beings are very visual, we need to do things in our worship that is visual. There are arguments of whether to have a screen in worship certainly deal with questions of tradition and appropriateness. But at the same time we want to communicate the Gospel to new people and we can do it effectively through pictures and words made clear and strong and through music, feeling, emotion and drama. God has given us different senses, and all of those senses are ways to communicate the faith. The Church needs to be a leader that leads in communicating the truth of Jesus Christ through all the senses and all the means. Any elementary school teacher understands learning theory and how people learn. It seems ridiculous that the church made up of educated people, many of them teachers, has too often neglected completely to use learning theory in the way we communicate the Gospel. We expect everyone to learn in some kind of logical sequential way and yet learning theory explains that many people only learn through experience. Public schools have labs, discussion and involvement projects. Too often the church is afraid of any innovation that uses a common and logical learning theory. We need to be leaders who communicate. We need to use all the learning theories in our leading and teaching. Jesus taught with pictures, metaphors, stories, object lessons and live demonstrations. The church needs to lead effectively. To provide worship that connects the individual with God, to provide worship that is meaningful and instructs the Christian how to live, to provide worship that gives the opportunity to build strong community and fellowship, to provide worship that celebrates our commitment to Jesus Christ as Lord and Savior–these are our goals. We are called to do them effectively.

The Purpose of the Church

The church's call is to lead–lead in teaching the faith, lead in making the world better, lead in organizing the community and lead in meeting the needs of the people. We are to be a Good Samaritan Church, and wherever there is a need, hurt or problem we should be there to help with the love and truth of Christ. So it is with helping people who have not known Christ to come to know Christ. The church's leadership needs to be one that is invitational and friendly, providing community groups, sharing times and discipleship studies that provide a way for the novice Christian to grow and the searching seeker to learn.

The church is called to lead in every way possible to help people to understand, know, live and share the Gospel of Jesus Christ. We ask our individual church members to take leadership and invite their friends to church to show hospitality and love, but all too often the church itself is cold, unfriendly and irrelevant. The church should use every means within the church and within the community to exercise its leadership in helping people know about Christ. This means we need to embrace advertising, media, publicity and event evangelism in the most professional, authentic and quality way we can. The community should know where the church stands on issues and what the church does. We understand clearly that it is important for a new department store in the community to spend a large amount of its budget on advertising, catalogs and descriptions of what they do. Yet we expect that a predominately non-Christian, secular community will know what the church is about, believes and does without ever using the media or simple communications avenues. We smile at the clever techniques and the clear way advertising is done. Super Bowl ads become more popular than the game because we believe in the communication that is involved in those ads, yet the church refuses to use most of these techniques in letting the world know what it is about. If we are going to take leadership and expect our members to be invitational, the church needs to stop being so cold, unfriendly, austere, uninvolved and primitive in our communications.

We expect the church member to explain to his friend what the church is as he makes an invitation. The church should be there to back up those stories by presenting the story of what it believes to the community in a clear, authentic way. Too much of a pastor's time and too much of local church business meetings are spent on aspects of the church that are more for the comfort of the members than they are for hospitality. It is time for the church to lead people to Jesus Christ as a priority.

Churches lead in many different ways. One of the ways to provide leadership is in the community. To lead like the Good Samaritan is the model for our church life—to be ready to help wherever the need, hurt or problem is; to stop beside the road, as the Good Samaritan did, take the risk and make the commitment to make a difference, do God's work and make things better. This is our task. A local church may be involved in helping with community problems, such as poverty and racial injustice and may provide leadership to support projects and organizations that are meeting needs of people in the community, such as Habitat for Humanity or the local food bank. The church, in providing these projects, services and help, shows how Christ's message affects our lives in positive ways. The church also leads by providing social networking that clearly exemplifies the message of Jesus Christ. The use of a Facebook page and other aspects of the Internet provide an opportunity for the church to share the truth and provide leadership in the community. The events that a church may do and the classes the church offers both provide ways in which the church helps the community.

During difficult economic times, a particular local church organized a program to help people out of work find jobs, prepare résumés and deal with the issue of unemployment. The community was impressed by the church's leadership, which showed that Christ's message is one that helps us deal with problems and issues. Another church organized a health clinic for those in the community that were facing economic difficulty as a way of showing that the followers of Christ are concerned about both physical and spiritual needs and hurts as well as health.

The worship services themselves and the things that the church proclaims in its worship are ways of showing that the church is providing leadership for the community. Taking stands on issues of human need, human rights, family values, morality, integrity and justice can show that a church cares and is willing to stand up for what's right, just as Jesus did.

Ask for Commitment to Christ

When I was a boy the churches in my small, rural Oklahoma town often had revivals. We all knew what it was about. It was organized for two purposes—spiritual renewal for church members and for people who didn't know Christ to make the commitment to accept Him as Lord and Savior. The business of the revival was to save souls and to revive and renew the church members. At the end of every evangelistic revival meeting there was a call. Would you accept Jesus Christ as your Lord and Savior? You were asked to "come forward"—get out of your pew or chair and walk to the front of the room. That was the physical sign that you wanted to commit to Jesus Christ.

Today we rarely have revival meetings. Few churches have an altar call. Decisions to follow Christ are made in the comfort of the pastor's study or in a meeting where you can fill out a card and make the decision. Those techniques work and many people appreciate the fact they can make the decision quietly in a logical, non-emotional way. Too often the problem is that we do not provide opportunities for people to make their commitment in a way that is clear and decisive and shows our determination to make a difference. It is ironic that, in a world where people show great enthusiasm and loyalty at sporting events and trends and fashions in dress and behavior are so pervasive, we seem to be reluctant to be open and demonstrate the depth of our commitment to Jesus Christ. Certainly, cognitive, quiet, dignified expressions of commitment are valid, but our culture is one that is often extremely demonstrative and we need to be willing and comfortable, allowing our commitment to Christ to be emotional, public and passionate just as it is deep, logical and caring.

In a culture that has become confused about religion, some people want to become spiritual in a rather controlled environment. But if we expect the individual Christian to invite their friends not only to come to church but to follow Jesus, we should provide many different ways to make the commitment. If we expect grandparents to have enough courage to talk to their grandson about Jesus and salvation, shouldn't the church be willing to talk about commitment clearly and without apology? Leading is inviting some person seeking to follow Christ without apology.

Our commitment to Jesus Christ is the very heart of who we are, the very definition of our personalities, goals and direction. Therefore, what we say and do as a church ought to point to that commitment. Though methods of expressing ideas change, our articulating of the commitment to Jesus Christ should not be compromised, diminished or held back. Too many times, pastors and church leaders feel like a church becomes more attractive when it makes fewer requests of commitment. Lav Schauer once wrote of a parallel between high-demand churches and voluntary association churches. High-demand churches were clear about responsibilities and the purpose and direction of the church. Voluntary associations were unclear; they made few requests, demands and requirements for a person to be a part of the church. Schauer's research indicated that churches that grew were the high-demand churches; churches that lost their strength in the community were the voluntary association churches.

However we describe it, the church is called to be clear about its purpose, goals and requirements. Therefore, the church should never compromise in the insistence upon its members and friends making a commitment to Jesus Christ. Commitment is a way in which we mobilize our energies, clarify our attitudes and beliefs and direct our strategic planning. Though we may not hold the same kind of revival meetings we once held, our commitment to calling people to accept Jesus Christ as Lord and Savior needs to not be compromised in any kind of way. The way a local church publicly expresses its purpose and mission, describes its identity and publicizes its activities should never compromise its call to commitment to Jesus Christ.

Church Unity to Share the Faith

The Church often finds itself battling between denominations and doing spiritual warfare between the liberals and the conservatives. Most of the time these battles among the groups within the church have done nothing more than create a continual lack of integrity within the church and provide ammunition for the critics of Christian commitment. We have spent our time as Christian church leaders being angry at the other side rather than being concerned about the sins of the world. We have more passion and energy criticizing our fellow Christians than we do in leading our agnostic friends to know the love of God.

So many Christian leaders spend more time criticizing their fellow clergy than working together to lead people to Christ. So much energy is spent when denominations argue about their differences rather than working together to lead people to a way of love and peace. It would seem almost silly for Christians in this very secular world to become so involved criticizing other followers of Jesus and using our energy to express that criticism when the secular world sees us as irrelevant and uncaring. Since the beginning of the Church, we've had disagreements and differences and yet, when those disagreements and differences hamper our ability to mobilize the Church for God's work, they become our sin. It's time for us to repent and change. We as a Church need to be united together. Paul recognized in the twelfth chapter of First Corinthians that we are different; we have different functions as part of the body, but yet we are all one with Christ, the Head. This must be our priority.

We don't have the luxury of fighting each other any longer, but we have the privilege of learning the strength of the various forms of Christianity and the power of our unity together to lead new people to Christ. Today the Church needs to openly and actively affirm that its agenda is to lead people to become fully devoted followers of Jesus Christ rather than spend our energy criticizing each

199

other. Paul taught in First Corinthians, *"For just as the body is one and has many members, and all the members of the body, though many, are one body, so it is with Christ"* (12:12 ESV).

Conclusion

Certainly the other aspects of the church's life are important and they are functional to this primary purpose. Worship services, pastoral care, community service, Christian education and social justice are all important aspects of the church's life, but it is time that the goal of making disciples becomes first on our to do list. We must be clear to the secular world and unapologetic to persons of various religious and non-religious points of view. We are the Church and our task is making disciples of Christ.

Questions for Discussion and Personal Reflection

1. Consider how leading people to Christ is the main function of the organized church.

2. Consider why and how individuals should work together as the church in order to lead people to Christ.

3. In the second chapter of Acts are the stories how the early Christians told the story of Jesus and how they ask people to join the church. Consider how the Church today can lead others to Christ.

4. Give some examples of how the church's teaching, programs, or activities help people to find Christ. Is your church invitational?

5. Tell a story of how a particular activity of the church has really helped a person to change and become a follower of Christ.

6. Discuss the most effective ways to invite someone to church.

7. Review the aspects of your worship service, asking how it relates to the love of Christ—how warm, friendly and helpful are your worship services?

8. Does your church emphasize commitment to Jesus Christ as Lord and Savior? How clear is that commitment made and how strong is it emphasized?

9. Spend a few moments in prayer then consider a program or a plan for how a church would really become an evangelistic center and a community influence to Christ?

Chapter 18
Fishing and Family

When I was a boy, my father loved to go fishing. We lived a rural, sometimes very dry area of Oklahoma, where the fishing places were very limited. We could fish on my grandfather's farm in the farm ponds made by the small creek that ran through his cattle pasture. We could fish on the Canadian River, but most of the time the Canadian was not running, so the fish were in a few of the ponds along the river. We dreamed of a time we might go to Colorado and fish in the mountain streams. There are many lakes in Oklahoma, built to protect the state from periodic floods. They were great places to spend a day with your dad fishing. I suppose there were times that in my fantasies I might have dreamed of going deep sea fishing, but no one in my family ever had. As a boy learning how to fish and I realized there were lots of places to catch fish.

So it is with being fishermen working for Jesus. The world is our parish, therefore all the ponds are possible places to share our faith and lead people to find the joyful power of Jesus Christ in their lives. This chapter is about fish ponds, lakes and rivers and how to fish in all the different places.

The Fishing Metaphor

Jesus lived in the first century in a land where grain was sown by throwing it on the bare land. The farming techniques had not yet developed with much sophistication. Fishing was done in simple ways with nets and fishing, like farming, was a concept that everyone understood. Today fishing is seen as something different than the first century; it is mostly a sport or recreation. So for some people the metaphor may not work, but its simplicity and biblical foundation is worth our remembering.

Fishing in Three Places

One of the theories of human relationships used by sociologists is that we have three places that we live in life. One is in the family, the second is the workplace and the third is the social place–neighbors, circle of friends, local bar, church or wherever we find community outside of the workplace and home.

In this section of the book, I want to talk about fishing in the family, workplace and the third place, where you have relationships provide–some are deep and clear while others are vague, passing and superficial. The three places are real and opportunities to go fishing.

Relationships

The first characteristic of being able to fish is having an opportunity to build a relationship, whether it is in the family, at your local civic center, with the guy at the office next to yours, with another teacher in your school system or with neighbors. These are all opportunities to share the faith. The first, most critical step in sharing the faith is to build relationships that are authentic. Too many times we try to share the faith in a superficial way where the relationship is not Christ-like, loving, caring and sharing. We share like a used car salesman, and it doesn't work. People see through our falseness; we seem superficial when we share Christ. At an office party where there is some remark about our church, without understanding who we are talking to or what is going on, we often say the wrong thing instead of the right. We need to know who we are talking to. We need to know who we are relating to whether family or friends.

Witnessing begins with a good relationship of love. We need to build relationships. Jesus cared; Jesus taught us sensitivity. Paul in discussing First Corinthians 13 laid out a series of guidelines for relations. Those guidelines must be guidelines that are used in sharing the faith. To paraphrase Paul, love—and thus evangelism—is patient and kind; it is not jealous or boastful, arrogant or rude. It doesn't insist upon its own way or get angered easily. It doesn't delight in evil but rejoices with the truth. It focuses on truth, hope and perseverance. We need to learn that gentle kind of evangelism that is built upon a loving relationship. We as Christians need to be the most Christ-like we can be. We need to allow the spirit of Jesus Christ to live in us in such a vital way that everybody who meets us and knows us experiences Christ's love. Family, friends and acquaintances should think there is something really different about us and know that difference is Jesus Christ.

Fishing in the Family

One of the greatest opportunities for evangelism in a highly secular world is our own family. They are the first place we should share the faith. Because you have experienced the joy, meaning and purpose in following Jesus Christ, those persons who we love the most should be the first place we share. The problem is that often times there are resentments, obligations, roles and expectations that make the family a difficult place to share the faith. There are family loyalties that oftentimes make it difficult and yet it is the closest and most relevant place for us to share the faith in Jesus Christ. So how do we fish in the family?

In using the simple acrostic of TELL as the lens to plan our strategy, begin with T. One of the most obvious ways we can tell the story of Jesus is through the truth of our own lives. That means knowing what we believe in and standing up for it, being clear about the values that Jesus taught and letting those values dictate our behavior. Hypocrisy is the greatest criticism leveled today towards the Christian community by the secular society, and we must be the first to stand against that hypocrisy and be people of faith no matter what. The stories of people being saints of the church on Sunday morning and the worst of sinners on Saturday night touches the children, skeptics and vulnerable ones in our families first. When a child sees his dad angry and out of control over a simple argument or problem in the family on Saturday night and then piously sitting in worship or teaching a Sunday school class on Sunday morning, there is skepticism about the Christian faith that is all too embarrassing.

Know that the family is watching you. We need to be clear about what we believe, centered on the truth of Jesus Christ in our own lives, and willing to share and tell it. In the stories told around the dinner table, stories told during holidays or at times of crisis, we have a great opportunity to explain what we believe in, what we stand for and who we are. The truth of our experience in Jesus Christ should come out in the way we raise children, deal with crisis and make decisions. We need to do our best sharing of our faith in the family. That is not to say we have to hide our own weakness, but we need to find our own strength and learn the appropriate ways to admit our faults, deal with our weaknesses, confess our sin, repent and change our ways. The truth of our behavior becomes so evident in the family. If we are authentic, honest, committed and caring, we can powerfully lead others to Christ. If we are inauthentic and hypocritical we become detrimental to our family members following Christ.

The E reminds us to explain. The family provides great opportunities to explain. We use conversations, arguments and discussions as ways to explain what Jesus said and what He taught. We must become well trained theologians of Jesus Christ. We cannot hang on to old clichés and irrelevant ways of speaking about the faith and be able to teach our children and our relatives what the way of Jesus Christ is. The authoritarian way of "do it because I say so" doesn't always work today. The answer is doing it because it is right and because of who Jesus Christ is. We need a foundation of

Christian explaining. Too often parents can't explain why or how. Too often the doubting cousin who visits for Christmas is never given the opportunity to hear your story of the love of God and beauty of Christmas because we never even think to explain that Christmas is more than gifts under the tree. We need to become natural theologians who can explain to a very skeptical family.

The first L in the TELL story reminds us of how important our example of living is. In the paragraphs that I have written about the truth in your life, I have reminded us that behavior is the truth. It is the first way we show our faith. We need to live the faith. We need to be living examples of Jesus Christ. When the secular twenty-something nephew in your family is caught in a difficult time and is trying to decide who he can talk to about it, our goal should be to be the first person that he thinks of. We should be the trusted listeners because of our love, concern and sensitivity. We need to show Christ to our family.

The second L reminds us of leading. No matter your role in the family—the youngest child or the oldest adult—you are called to be a leader who does the extra things to help people know about Christ. Leading can be done by encouraging a teenager to go to a youth program, sharing the love of the church with a niece going through divorce or explaining God's forgiveness to a teenager who has behaved very badly. We need to be leaders who invite, encourage, pray for and use our relationships within the family. We should do this to help our loved ones to experience Jesus Christ in whatever way we can and any situation possible.

Whether it is inviting a relative who hasn't been to church in years to the Christmas Eve candlelight service or inviting your 10-year-old grandson who hasn't been to church since he was five to spend the summer with you and learn about Jesus, we are called to be leaders. The family is our first place of fishing.

Christian fishing isn't just catching, it is helping someone find Jesus Christ and become a full-fledged disciple. Truth, explaining, living and leading are words that describe not only catching, but cultivating, growing, disciplining and helping your family members become strong, fully devoted followers of Jesus Christ who join you in the task of fishing.

Questions for Discussion and Personal Reflection

1. Consider the three places the theory of our lives: family, work and friends.
2. Share ways in which you have shared the faith within your family.
3. What are some of the difficulties of witnessing within our own family?
4. What are the basic responsibilities of being a member of a family such as a parent or grandparent and the task of sharing the faith?
5. Consider what are the basic principles or guidelines you should use in sharing your faith within your family.
6. Take a few moments to pray for your family, particularly those who have not accepted Christ.
7. Develop a strategy for how you will become a better witness for Christ in your family. Detail the schedule in terms of strategy for witnessing to particular people.

Chapter 19
Fishing in the Second and Third Place

The second place is described by sociologists as the place we work. The other fellowship environments such as clubs, gyms, church and volunteer organizations–the places that we find community are sometimes called the third place. This chapter is dedicated to helping us to review how to share our faith in the second and third places.

The key to sharing the faith is to listen and really know the other person. It is to be like Jesus and really care. The key to being able to share is listening. We must know, remember and love the other person.

It then begins with our own experience, our truth, that is, the truth of what God has done for us in Jesus Christ. We are not selling a car, a vacation package or a new pair of shoes; we are introducing people to the experience of Jesus Christ and we are doing it because we have experienced Christ in our own lives. That is the truth and our starting point. It is what makes us different, empowers our life and gives us purpose, satisfaction, direction, peace and a set of ethics by which to live. It is best understood in our own experience and own story. We begin with that point of view. Some evangelistic activities in the past began by focusing on the sinfulness of our friends. The reality of universal sinfulness was made clear by Paul as he reminded us that *"all have sinned and fallen short of the Glory of God"* (Romans 3:23). Rarely do we need convincing of this; it is evident all around us. However, to begin with someone's badness understandably puts them on the defensive and puts them down and raises us up. So the saint is telling the sinner, "Straighten up or you will go to hell." That concept might be right, but for the secular, self-centered individual in American society today, it only creates separation, not relationship. Your story of what God has done for you in Christ told enthusiastically and humbly without arrogance is the beginning point. We need to practice, think about and study our story. How do we explain what God has done? How do we share the joy of following Christ? This truth is where we begin.

They both worked for the city crew that repaired streets. In between jobs they talked. The whole crew talked off and on about everything including scores of games, the idiosyncrasies of their boss, television programs, movies and many personal, individual topics. Nate noticed that Frank participated a little differently than some of the others did in the group. Nate never remembered Frank telling a dirty joke. He was a real friend to everyone. Frank listened and cared. He was kind in his conversation, not rude or arrogant, and at the same time really firm. He had some beliefs that Nate admired. Frank seemed to be the only guy that cared about what was right and fair. Everybody else on the crew was just out for themselves. Nate wished he was more like Frank. One day they were sitting together eating their lunch on a small bench near the worksite. Frank took the opportunity to speak up, "Frank, what do you have that gives you such a sense of integrity? You really care about people. I admire you sometimes; with all the crap that we talk about and things we say, I am a little ashamed. Why are you so different?" Frank was a little embarrassed. He was a pretty bashful guy, but he realized this was the opportunity he had been waiting for. He thought carefully and began to explain that in recent years he had searched for something to really build his life around. He wanted more meaning and purpose than just working on the street crew. He had started going to church and he had found Christ. Christ had given him a new attitude, sense of peace and power. Nate was a little put off about what Frank was saying, but Frank was so sincere. For the rest of that lunch and the next five or six lunches they talked about faith. Mostly, Nate asked questions about Jesus and what it means to trust in God. How do you become a Christian? What is the church? Frank answered every one of Nate's questions carefully, as best he could.

A few weeks later, after Nate had attended a couple of Sundays with Frank at church, his pastor stopped him in the hallway and told him how pleased he was that Nate was coming. Frank stopped for a moment and said, "You know I want to thank you for that sermon series you did in the spring about the basics of our faith." Frank cleared his throat and continued, "You were questioning whether we needed to know the basics again." He then said what most pastors need to hear: "We desperately need to know them. The questions that people ask us today must have good answers. There is so much crap being said about Christianity." As he used the word he felt a little embarrassed saying that to his pastor. He kind of stepped back and said, "No I really mean it that way, it is crap! We need the basics. We need to know what we believe in, what we stand for, what is the truth." Then Frank said with the kind of enthusiasm that wasn't his natural way of approaching things, "Thanks for the sermon series, for being a teaching pastor and caring about the truth." Then Frank said to the pastor something that all of us need to hear: "If we are expected to witness to our faith today, we have to know simple answers. The old clichés will not work. We need new words, clear explanations, logical descriptions and a strong Biblical foundation."

This story of Nate, Frank and the pastor is a story of the struggle we have today in dealing with the "E" part of sharing our faith. We need to listen. We need to explain and explain and explain. We need to counter the confusion and unhealthy descriptions of Christianity that are promoted and believed by so many within our society. To share to the people in our third place, we have to be informed and educated theologians. We must be educated about our faith, and how to share our faith, so that we can answer questions clearly and effectively. In a secular culture, those elementary questions must be answered because there are so many misunderstandings present around us. We must be educated about the culture, mindset and contemporary self-centered philosophies and be able to respond clearly and helpfully.

The third part of sharing the faith to people of the second and third places of our lives has to do with simply living it. Like the story of Nate and Frank they will see by the way you live and make decisions, by what you don't do or say, by what you stand up for and by what you refuse to agree with. The "L" stands for living and it is by living that the truth is known about Christ.

Everyone in the neighborhood knew that Tim and Allison and their children attended church. They were unapologetic about their faith. Tim often talked about his commitment to Christ, the things he and his family did in the church and what they believed. It wasn't obnoxious, just truthful. At the same time, everyone knew Tim and Allison just didn't seem to get along. They had conflicts on everything! It was oftentimes embarrassing in the neighborhood, at a sporting event or just while working in the yard they got into loud disagreements. They were honest about it and went to counseling, talked to their pastor and tried hard to make their marriage work. One night Tim become so agitated over some conflict between the two of them that he lost control. He hit her more times than anyone would want to remember. The police were called, and she was taken to the emergency room. They separated and eventually divorced.

We all understand there are times that even the best of us get out of control. Yet, when we set an example that is contrary to the way of Christ, our witness goes down the drain. When it is like it was for Tim, every positive thing that he had tried to do about sharing the faith with his wife, children and neighbors was contradicted. The neighbors talked about this "blowhard Christian" who seemed to be so pious but really was a dirty rat. The children caught in the hurtful middle talked about their daddy and what he did to their mom.

Our behavior reveals so much. Living the faith is critical and helps others understand the power of Jesus Christ. At the same time, those mistakes we make, whether it is abuse of the family, an inappropriate joke or unkind language, provide fuel for those who see Christians as hypocrites. The modern post-Christian era has created an environment where what Christians do, speak so much louder than what they say. The negative things the Christian does get much more attention than the positive things. It is a sad commentary about our human nature that mistakes, even though they may be regretted later, become so detrimental. Committed Christians must understand that action is loud and obvious. We must be men and women who show our faith in love and in our families who are the example of Jesus Christ in business dealings, relationships and casual conversations. It means that while there are appropriate times to take a stand and be clear, there are also appropriate times to be quiet and wait for another opportunity. We must exercise wisdom in all we do, thereby showing the power of Christ in the way we live. We must be strategic, sensitive, knowledgeable and discreet. In dealing with family and friends, the positive action teaches so much. The person who goes the extra mile to help, the friend who is there in times of trouble and the business associate who refuses to go along with an illegal deal all set an example of the power of Jesus Christ that cannot be missed. These are times in this post-Christian area when behavior matters.

The last "L" stands for lead. In previous times, leading was the first thing we did. We made the invitation. We stated an accusation. We condemned. We criticized and we encouraged. These overt actions of leadership must be done today, but they must be done carefully. Witnessing needs to be done with the sensitivity of the Holy Spirit as we invite someone to church, invite a friend to a church related activity, talk to a business associate about a moral principle or share our story among a group of friends. We are called to lead by inviting people to know Christ, know the church and attend the services and programs. We are called to lead people to find the joy that we find. It may take a few moments of conversation or it may take several years, but we are never encouraged to give up. We are always called to continue to lead persons to Jesus Christ.

To lead a person to Christ, today more than ever, we need to listen carefully first. We do this to understand our friends, family and coworkers. The opportunities to lead in the workplace and in the place of fellowship are usually riddled with the possibility of making serious mistakes. We can offend a friend, upset a coworker or create a feeling of suspicion, arrogance, judgment and cruelty so easily because people often expect Christians to be arrogant, insensitive and judgmental. Our behavior is thought and understood that way even though we mean it totally differently. The way to guard against that misunderstanding is to listen and understand how the person we are speaking to really feels and what they have gone through. If we were missionaries in another culture on another continent, we would first learn about the people and learn their feelings, thoughts, prejudices and preconceived ideas in order to communicate the truth of Jesus Christ. So it is in leading in the workplace and among so many of our friends and associates. We need to listen before we speak.

Edgar and Lou had been coworkers at the post office for years. They had worked up through the ranks and now they were assigned to a project where they needed to work together. Their task was to last a couple of years or longer. They came to associate regularly and often. They liked each other and got along together well. Lou quickly began to realize that Edgar had some pretty strong negative feelings about church and about "church people." They were good friends, and Lou naturally wanted to lead his friend Edgar to find the joy and happiness that he had found in Christ. So often as they worked, an opportunity for Lou would come up where he could speak a word about faith, belief, conviction or the church. He was so ready to do that and yet Lou felt it was simply the wrong time. So he began to listen to his friend Edgar as he shared in casual or frustrated moments. Lou soon learned that Edgar had been brought up in a Christian home with parents who had gotten divorced. His mother remarried, and Edgar's stepfather was a deeply committed, radical, conservative Christian Evangelical. He was determined that Edgar would be a Christian like him. He taught, yelled at and punished Edgar. Edgar was forced to go to church, be baptized and go to certain kinds of evangelical activities, and Edgar resolved that his stepfather was a mean man—mean as a father and mean to his mother. Edgar decided he would never be like that man. Lou realized that most anything that he might have said normally to Edgar might trigger a negative reaction, so he carefully talked about his faith. He chose his language well, not using old clichés that would bring up bad memories. He talked candidly about hypocrisy in the church and the world in a way that opened the topic to his friend Edgar. One day a significant breakthrough happened. Something had come up about an evangelistic meeting that Lou attended, and Edgar simply asked if he could talk to Lou about the faith. He said he knew that Lou was a deeply committed Christian and he had never had a friend that he would trust as much as he did Lou. He said how much he appreciated Lou's convictions, sensitivity, fairness and honesty, and he wondered if they could talk about faith. Lou carefully entered into the discussion for he knew that certain words and examples were loaded with bitter feelings for Edgar. He had to lead with gentle care and honesty. This conversation was the first of many. There were times that Lou felt like he was Edgar's therapist. There were times that Lou went to his pastor, himself a good counselor, and they talked about how to understand what Edgar had been through.

Eventually there was a late afternoon when they were leaving the post office. Edgar had been extra quiet that day. As they left Edgar said he was afraid. Lou said, "What are you afraid of?" Edgar said that he wanted so much to be like Lou and to be a loving Christian but he didn't want to be like his stepdad. He was afraid to really commit. It was a breakthrough. They both stood in the parking lot and cried. Two weeks later Lou, Edgar and the pastor met for lunch. The conversation went on for some time, and eventually Edgar recommitted his life to Christ. This time, he gave himself through the leadership of his good friend Lou in joy and total free will. This is a story that needs to remind us of how to lead. We need to lead with care, thoughtfulness, knowledge and conviction. Our goal is too precious to allow us to be ignorant about how to lead someone to Jesus Christ today.

The real place of leading people to Christ today for most is the workplace and the social places. It is where we meet people who are struggling, open, afraid and closed, and help them to know Jesus Christ as Lord and Savior. With friends and acquaintances, we have the greatest opportunities. The old slogan, "Each one reach one" becomes most viable in the second and third place and it is where we can most often make serious mistakes. We need to be, as the Bible says, *"wise as serpents and innocent as doves"* (Matt.10:16 ESV).

Questions for Discussion and Personal Reflection

1. Take a few moments and describe the kinds of people that you know at work or among your friends who do not know Christ.
2. Take a moment and describe some categories of unbelieving people you know, such as the disappointed, angry, hurt and searching. Describe the characteristics of these categories then think about how you would help people with these characteristics know Christ.
3. List some of the roadblocks to sharing the faith. What are some things in our contemporary society among our friends and coworkers that make it difficult to share the faith?
4. Discuss strategies to overcome these difficulties.
5. If applicable, think and share the story of when you have been able to successfully lead a friend or a coworker to Christ. What happened?
6. What are some of the hard questions that are asked of you when you are leading secular acquaintances to Christ? Make a list of people who are friends or coworkers that you want to lead to Christ and begin to pray for them.

Chapter 20
Christ's Church

For over 30 years, I served as pastor of a church in Tulsa, Oklahoma. The church was started in 1954 in the midst of suburban growth in the city of Tulsa. When I came much later to serve, it was now midtown and in a declining neighborhood. In 1954, the charter members of the church needed to name it. They considered lots of names, but the name they eventually decided upon was Christ Church. The names of churches vary with the culture, neighborhood, landmarks and countless other things, and I felt it was a distinctive blessing for the church to be called Christ United Methodist Church.

There is no better name than being a Christ church. Denominations have named themselves in all kinds of ways, trying to articulate their beliefs just like retail establishments try to convey what they sell or do by their name. It would seem to me that whatever the name is on the front sign, churches need to be a Christ church. Often, people accept Jesus Christ as their Lord and Savior and are excited about growing in the faith and becoming fully devoted followers, but the church sometimes lets them down. The effectiveness of the local church is so often the key to the Christian's healthy spiritual growth. Reaching new people for Christ is directly related to the health and effectiveness of the church.

This book has described the task of individuals and the Church in sharing the faith. Christianity is not a by yourself kind of task; it is done in community with friends and fellowship. The story of the beginning of the early Church found in the book of Acts is the story of people committed to each other and to God, people seeing themselves as the Body of Christ.

Today, and in other generations in the past, we felt the church needed to be renewed; it needed to regain what it was created for. So reformers and renewalists have sought to bring the Church back to Jesus Christ over and over. They've used all kinds of words, descriptions, liturgies and even music to do it. Sometimes these worked and renewal happened. Sometimes it did not. I believe the key to the power of the church is not the music or the liturgies or all the other aspects. The key is that the church is being Christ-centered.

We cannot think about how to share the faith unless we at the same time are committed to keeping the church strong with valid principles while being attractive to new people. The church must organize programs and practices that help people grow in the faith and lead worship in forms that build spiritual strength. Principles of witnessing, sharing, leading people to Christ and following the divine imperative of Jesus must include a commitment to keeping the church Christ-like. The following pages are not about church government or polity; they have nothing to do with liturgy or style of music; they are not about the ordination of clergy, the form of baptism or procedures for the sacrament of Holy Communion. To be a church effective in reaching new people authentically, we must be Christ-centered. To be a Christ church, there are certain things that we need to do and be, certain things we need to believe and practice that are beyond liturgy or polity, but are basic for helping the new Christian grow and be empowered to reach others. Every Christian leader has a set of principles that they think are the key to the renewed church. The following are mine. I believe these principles are necessary for the church to be effectively evangelical.

1. Jesus Christ Is the Absolute Center

There are so many doctrines, procedures and emphases that consume the life of the church, but, if they're not Christ-centered, we get taken off on tangents, emphasizing things that don't matter and that are linked to culture and personal idiosyncrasies. When Charles Sheldon wrote his book, *In His Steps*, in 1896, he presented a theological concept that the church is the group of people who are asking, "What would Jesus do?" in every decision they make as a Church or as individuals. That is, the Church is Christ-centered in its behavior, commitment and theology. I have called it "Christyle." In the gospels of Jesus Christ, the writers are clear about what it means to follow Jesus. We need to have that same commitment. Whatever the liturgical language we use, the harmony of music that's popular or the government forum that is required, the real requirement is Jesus Christ. Christ is the standard of what we do, the motivation for what we do and the explanation for what we do. If people in the community do not see Jesus Christ in what we do as a church, then all the witnessing is simply some kind of sales talk to get members of our organization. The Church is the Church of Jesus Christ. Paul called it the "body of Christ" in Romans 12. Peter said the Church is "in his steps" (1 Peter 2:21). John calls us to "abide in him" (1 John 2:6).

In Luke 10, Jesus describes clearly what this means as He presents the Great Commandments: loving God with our heart, mind, soul and body and loving our neighbors as ourselves. There are three dimensions of this following Jesus Christ that are made clear in the Great Commandments; one is love towards God; the second is love towards others; the third is love towards ourselves. Each point of this triangle of loving relationships compliments the others. It is out of our love for others that we show our love for God; it is because God loves us so much that we can love ourselves despite our sin. As you show love so you experience the power of God in your life. Charles Sheldon used First Peter 2:21 as his branding scripture to describe what it means to follow in the steps of Jesus. We too must follow First Peter 2:21, which reads, *"To this you were called, because Christ suffered for you, leaving you an example, that you should follow in his steps,"* as our marching orders. Jesus made it clear Himself, if you are to be His disciples, you *"must take up [your] cross daily and follow [Him]"* (Luke 9:23).

2. We Must Meet the Needs of Others

The only parable that Jesus told where He told us, "Go and do the same thing" is the parable of the Good Samaritan, found in Luke 10 following the Great Commandments. Jesus tells us who our neighbor is: It is anyone in need. Jesus described His own ministry and what He wanted to do when He went to His hometown of Nazareth following His baptism. He took the Scriptures that day and read what is recorded in Luke 9, *"'The Spirit of the Lord is on me, because he has anointed me to proclaim good news to the poor. He has sent me to proclaim freedom for the prisoners and recovery of sight for the blind, to set the oppressed free, to proclaim the year of the Lord's favor'"* (Luke 9:18–19). We are to respond wherever the needs and hurts are. Today, church renewal will come when churches become more concerned about others than they are about themselves. As we are concerned about the hurts and needs of others, we lead others to following Jesus. The best method of evangelism is based upon the needs of the other person. The needs of people at our point in history may be created by certain phenomena within our culture or society. The needs will change as the situations change, but the call to help, care, redeem and lead are always there. Paul makes it clear in the eighth chapter of Romans that nothing will separate us from the love of God in Christ Jesus our Lord, so we are to show that love to everyone we see.

3. We Must Be Loving

Paul was writing to the church in Corinth; they obviously were having some troubles. He describes the church as the body of Christ:

different parts, same head; different functions, same goal (1 Cor. 12:12). In Romans 12:5, he tells the church at Rome how to treat each other and says, "We are members one of another." In the thirteenth chapter, Paul summarizes it, saying, *"All the law and all the prophets can be summarized in the simple commandment to love your neighbor"* (Rom. 13:9).

First Corinthians 13 is not just a beautiful poem to be read at weddings, but it is a description of how Christians are to behave every day, all the time, without exception. If Christ is in you, others will see the love of Christ in the way you behave. The criticisms of the Church today are that it is hypocritical, arrogant and even mean. These are a condemnation upon our inability to live the life of love that Jesus Christ demanded of us. We ought to be ashamed of our unloving behavior and commit ourselves never to be that way again. Instead, to paraphrase First Corinthians, the church is patient and kind; the church is not jealous or boastful or proud. It does not dishonor others, it is not self-seeking, it is not easily angered, it keeps no record of wrongs. The church does not delight in evil but rejoices with the truth. It always protects, always trusts, always hopes, always perseveres.

4. Church Is God-Empowered

Paul's assurance in Romans 8 that nothing would ever separate us from the love of God is the way God wants it to be. However, we get distracted: we shut the door and fail to listen; we get so busy arguing about how to fix the toilet in the restroom at the church that we forget to listen to God about how lead people to Christ. We get so busy in the church managing our finances that we forget why we have any finances to start with.

The twenty-third Psalm is a beautiful poem that we read regularly at funerals. Its images of green pastures, still waters and the cup running over are beautiful metaphors. The psalmist says it clearly, "God is our shepherd." He is the boss; He is the one in control; He is your leader. It is easy for churches to be so busy doing their own thing–fighting for their own idiosyncrasies and raising money for their own pet projects–that they become functionally atheistic congregations. They function and live like they don't even know that God exists. They simply don't pay any attention to the power of God present in their church life, Scripture or Jesus.

We often wait for that moment of high inspiration; we climb a mountain and look to the sky and say, "Wow! God exists!" We hold a baby and say, "Thank you, God, for this new life." We go through a crisis and the doctor tells us that the cancer surgery was successful; they got it all. When we finish wiping the tears from our eyes, we might remember to thank God for what happened. Yet, in the ordinary things of life–driving a car down the street, missing breakfast when we're late to work or arguing with a fellow employee about the task that needs to be done–we never think about God! God is so patient with us when we are so unconcerned about the reality of our Creator. The most important characteristic of your church, if it is truly to be evangelistic, is that it is a "God place," where you teach about God and God's holy power in the lives of His people. The Church is where we teach that there are principles of truth that are recognized as God's principles in life, such as justice, truth, dignity, love and morality. The effective and healthy church is God-empowered and God-centered.

Sean and Freddy worked together at a car dealership for years. They were mechanics and good friends. Sean, in his own faith development, came to understand how precious it is to share our faith with others, and so he began the process of witnessing to his friend. Freddy was loud and sometimes a little obnoxious and didn't always listen carefully. It was hard for Sean to get Freddy's attention long enough for Freddy to understand what Sean felt was so important about Christ. But, finally, in the midst of some serious transitions that were happening in both of their lives, Freddy listened and changed. He accepted Christ and became a new person. Sean and Freddy's friendship deepened until Sean was transferred halfway across the country. They were both busy in their jobs and lost contact after a few years until Sean was transferred back, and they became friends again. Sean was brokenhearted when he realized what had happened to Freddy; it's true he'd become a Christian years before, but the church that he attended had forgotten about the four principles that I mentioned earlier. It was a fine institution; they collected pledges every year and built a new building once in a while, but they never built Christian character in Freddy's life, nor the lives of his wife and children. As Sean talked to Freddy again, he realized how sad it was that Freddy had not had a family of Christians who cared for, loved and supported him in his spiritual growth. The church had become just another social organization that Freddy belonged to, and, as time had gone on, Freddy and his family had discarded their loyalty because church didn't really seem to matter. When the church was started, they named it after the street; they called it the Fourteenth Street Church, and maybe that's all it ever was—a church building on Fourteenth Street that never made a real difference.

I pray that as you read this book about sharing the faith, your commitment to Christ becomes stronger than ever before and your commitment to being an evangelist for Christ becomes clear as can be. But there is another part of that commitment that must remain strong as well, and that is the commitment to keeping the church healthy, truly the body of Christ. May you be empowered to be a part of that body with integrity, passion and persistence.

Questions for Discussion and Personal Reflection

1. Reflect upon the ways that churches become identified. Emphasize certain aspects of their denomination, life or community that become their identity.
2. Think about some of the churches that you have attended in your life. What are the ways that people speak of them? What is their identity?
3. If we take the instruction by Jesus to take up our cross daily and follow Him to heart, how should a church behave?
4. List some of the characteristics of a church where Christ is the center, focus or standard. Reflect on what you can do personally to keep the church centered on Christ in its daily decisions and long-term goals.

Chapter 21
Everyone Is a Worker

Jesus used the metaphor of the harvest field as He called for people to do evangelism, *"The harvest is plentiful, but the workers are few"* (Matt. 9:37). The Church continually deals with the issue of too few laborers. The task of being responsible sometimes seems hard, the task of doing the right thing sometimes is avoided because it is perceived as being more difficult, so, in our world filled with difficulties and problems, it often seems like the need is great and the workers are few. Today, the field is ripe for the harvest. Our world is filled with people who are willing to do anything to find the pleasure that they are seeking. We live in a world that often seems unchristian, immoral, unjust and uncaring. The hurt this causes chaos, destruction, crisis and bewilderment. The need is so very great. The fields are ripe for the harvest.

The first two churches I served were right in the middle of the wheat farming area of Oklahoma. Though I had grown up with a farmer grandfather, the impact of harvest was never as clear as it is in the wheat farming belt across the country. When the wheat is ripe, it is a precarious time; a hail storm or torrential rain could come and ruin the crop. Other things can happen and lower the quality of the crop. The farmer knows, when the fields are white, it is time to cut the grain. Over the years, farmers have done many things to be efficient and effective at harvest time. They often hire all their friends and relatives to help harvest; they have all kinds of equipment to help them do the work. The mechanization of farming was to provide more labor and more effectiveness in responding to the ripeness of the wheat.

The Harvest Is Plentiful

Jesus pointed out that, when the time is right, it is time to respond. His metaphor was presented as an emergency–it is time! Right now! So it is for Christians to understand that now is the time. So many people are searching and hurting or becoming agnostic or atheistic; our culture is being influenced by a surge of atheism and an agnostic attitude in our society and by a secular culture that so often makes fun of Christians, points out their weaknesses and humanity. In the midst of this non-believing world, we need to understand that Jesus helps us to see this as an opportunity. Certainly, we want the society to be a "Jesus society," led by the rules of love, and yet when it is not, it is a new opportunity for Christians to share, tell the story and lead others to Christ. In the first century, Jesus said, "The fields are ripe for harvest." In the twenty-first century, it is obvious to all of us that the fields are indeed ripe.

Total Involvement

Because evangelism oftentimes seems difficult, it is often hard to recruit. Because evangelism has been done in ways that sometimes seem obnoxious, arrogant or uncaring, people make excuses about being available to do evangelism. Because evangelism takes lots of energy and sensitivity, people may help for a while but then quit. As I have taught about evangelism across the country, I find the most-asked questions are questions about recruiting help in doing local evangelism. There are two suggestions that I find we must use and understand. The first is the concept that every committed Christian must be a worker, a doer, involved. The second concept is that new members, new Christians, new followers of Jesus are sometimes the best, the most sensitive and should be asked as soon as they have made a commitment to be a part of the task of evangelism.

We must teach local church involvement over and over! Jesus' statement at Caesarea-Philippi about taking up our cross daily (Luke 9:24) is not an interesting alternative; it is the clear demand of being a Christian. We need to act. Jesus says in the Sermon on the Mount, *"Not everyone who says to me, 'Lord, Lord,' will enter the kingdom of heaven, but only he who does the will of my Father who is in heaven"* (Matt. 7:21). The emphasis is upon behavior. Paul describes the Church in the twelfth chapter of First Corinthians that everybody has a part. The jobs and roles are different, but everyone is a worker. This concept of total involvement must be taught over and over and over. The pressures of time, the confusion of priorities and the bewilderment of living in a society with a multiplicity of organizational demands create a difficult situation for the church to recruit leaders. There's always a reason why we can't help. Recruitment needs to be based more upon basic commitment than availability, since we're never really available. If we're committed to Jesus, we must be willing to be involved. Time is never easy to work out, but those who are committed to Jesus Christ will naturally find the time to do His work. The emphasis upon the Christyle as a behavioristic, theological approach places the center upon Christ and the response upon our action or behavior. Too many times, Christianity has just been a warm feeling. It is, as Jesus made it clear, a behavior. To follow Jesus is to be involved in His work in the church. There is no exception. Evangelism is obviously one of the priorities of the Church and our task as being followers must therefore include evangelism. If this is taught and expected by a local congregation; if every person who joins understands that involvement is an absolute necessity; if sermons include teachings on all of us being involved, then the task of recruitment for evangelism will not be an unpleasant burden of a few leaders but the joy of the church.

Recruiting the New Laborers

For all of us who have done recruitment in volunteer organizations, we realize that there is not always a certainty that people will volunteer. Some volunteer jobs are fun and others are not so fun; some we feel we have skills and talents for and others we feel are strange, even offensive. Those who have most recently given their lives to Christ tend to be the most enthusiastic, willing volunteers to lead others to Christ. Therefore, as we are recruiting new workers to lead people to Christ, the new Christians are the best workers and can be the most articulate witness! The recently changed agnostic, postmodern secularist can be most effective in leading other postmodern secularists to change and follow Christ. Some leaders of churches would not want to ask a new Christian to be on the evangelism team or invite the new member to be a greeter at the door. The committee would use words such as "give them a break," "give them a few years," "give them a chance to let them get better acquainted" or "don't be pushy with the new members."

People who become new members through needs-based evangelism are people who understand clearly that, to be a part of the church, you must be ready to go to work. They became new Christians because of a ministry. They expect to do ministry all of their lives. They signed up not because their best friends are there at the church or because it is prestigious to be a member of a particular church in the community; they are a part of the Christian community because they want to help. It was through ministry that they became fully devoted followers of Christ. It was by seeing the faith in action that they became part of the faith in action. It would be a contradiction to be only an audience member watching. It would be a radical contradiction if they became a part of the church and refused to lead and develop those very things that had led them to Christ. Some of our previous methods of personal evangelism were evangelism as "come and see," "it's a really big show" or "get a ticket to heaven." Though all of these descriptions may be true, the authentic and most powerful response that people have in becoming a follower of Christ is that, through your commitment, you become a doer in the Church of Christ.

Evangelism is an imperative for us today. There is one final part of this process of making a disciple, of leading someone to Christ. It is the exponential part of the story. We are called to share with someone else and help them find Jesus Christ in their life, and they are called to share with someone else and help them find Jesus Christ in their life, and they are called to share with someone else and help them find Jesus Christ in their life. This is not an interesting set of words to conclude this book; this is the description of what should happen. It is the exponential process. It's not just you leading someone to Christ, but they are leading someone to Christ and the process continues. Then, as you lead a second person, they lead a second, and a third, and a fourth and it grows. Like a geometric progression, the task of evangelism is a joyful increase of workers for God.

It may seem hard and difficult for us to share our faith in a way that's clear and strong. Yet when we experience the excitement of someone saying yes and accepting and following Christ, that is excitement! But it's just the beginning. One of the interesting things about becoming a Christian is that there seems to be a kind of satisfaction and fun that comes when we have made that decision for Christ. The effect of that is that we want to share with someone else. It is a strange reality that the most enthusiastic evangelists tend to be the newest Christians. Maybe it's because they understand how significant the change is, how really good it is, after years in the wilderness, to follow Christ after not following Christ.

There's a temptation of Christian leaders, when a new person has committed their life to Christ, to pat them on the back, tell them they're good and encourage them to rest for a while. Sometimes, a long while, not realizing we have taken the fun out of their experience, the joy out of their conviction, the momentum out of their life. The next sentence after welcoming someone into the faith following their baptism should be, "Would you like to come to the evangelism committee meeting next Tuesday night?" We need to understand the validity of passing it on, the satisfaction and the joy. The song *Pass It On* says it all. "It only takes a spark to get a fire going, and soon all those around can warm up in glowing. That's how it is with God's love—once you've experienced it, you spread His love to everyone; you want to pass it on.

Questions for Discussion and Personal Reflection

1. In our church, how do we recruit workers?
2. Do people who attend and join our church naturally want to help? Do we make it easy for them to volunteer?
3. What are some blocks that are created by the church that prevent people from becoming involved in the work of Christ through our local church?
4. Are there any traditions, practices or rules in our church life that make it difficult for someone to volunteer?
5. How can your church teach "total involvement?" How can we teach the "Christyle?"
6. How would we organize our church so that everyone would want to be involved and would stay involved?

Chapter 22
The Back Door

I have taught evangelism courses in churches all across the country; I have sat in pastors' offices and met with numerous church leaders, and oftentimes in the midst of a discussion, someone asks the question, "Certainly we need to make new disciples, but isn't it important we keep the ones we have? We lose so many people out the back door of the church. Shouldn't our emphasis be upon keeping what we have or at least trying to revitalize people whose names are still on our rolls but don't attend?" The answer is yes! We are concerned about everyone—including those who are members of the church but don't attend and those who have accepted Christ then become bewildered and leave the church by the back door.

How Do We Keep Our Members?

Often these remarks become an excuse for not doing evangelism as a church or as individuals. While we must be diligent so that this does not happen, the care for those who slipped away from the faith is very important. These key characteristics help achieve this:

1. **Discipleship Training:** An effective church needs a program of discipleship training so Christians become well trained and well equipped in the faith.

2. **Involvement:** A church must have a program of clear involvement so every church member understands their life is important in the church and they have a job or ministry to do. They are not just names on a roll, but they are a part of God's team.

3. **Care:** Churches need a care ministry that seeks to be there and mobilizes the help and health of the church for its

members when they face difficulties and problems. We
need to meet the needs of our own people as we meet the
needs of the community. The care program of the local
church needs to be a priority.

4. **Needs-Based Ministry:** Needs-based ministry is a way of
    talking about the life of the church that is relevant to the
    needs of the people in the ministry. Jesus Christ came out
    of God's love for each of us. When He died for our salva-
    tion, He showed how much God cares about our hurts,
    needs, growth, possibility and future. So the church needs
    to focus upon those needs. So often, the church becomes
    irrelevant, insensitive and out of touch with what's happen-
    ing in the culture, families and the local community. Pas-
    tors preach sermons that are hard to understand, boring
    and lacking direction or real help; Sunday school classes
    and programs of the church are biblically inept and not
    directed towards the real needs and issues of the commu-
    nity and our society. People within the church begin to feel
    that it is an irrelevant place, out of touch and that the Gos-
    pel of Jesus Christ does not make a difference. Churches
    need to focus upon the real needs of people, where they are
    and what's going on in their life. Our commitment is
    clearly to Jesus Christ, but our purpose is to lead people in
    becoming fully devoted followers. Responding to the place
    of need, hurt, trouble, difficulty, crisis or conflict is the way
    in which the Gospel of Jesus Christ brings God's love no
    matter what is happening.

Research on why people become inactive in church indicates
two primary reasons. One is some individual displeasure with the
life of the church, an angry situation, a hurt feeling that creates ani-
mosity or a separation. The second reason people become uninvolved and lose their vitality for the faith is because they go through
transitions. They become empty nesters, retire, serve in the military

or lose their job, and it is then the church's needs-based approach to ministry should be a primary focus. Through this approach, a church should be there as its members go through the ages and stages of life. God's love is there for us at every step of the way, and the church should be too. We in the church need to celebrate God's love and faithfulness in the way we organize our ministries so that the love is always there.

How to Develop Fully-Devoted Followers

The following four aspects of helping persons become followers of Christ are critically important: 1. discipleship training; 2. involvement; 3. care; and 4. needs-based ministry. These three become the antidote for people becoming disgruntled, confused or uninvolved. Each one of these programs needs to be a part of the outreach or evangelism program because they provide a natural, authentic grove for each person to remain in the reality and the power of the church. So often in the natural life of organizations, we become upset, angry, frustrated and bewildered at how others act or how the organization does things. This is sometimes because of our lack of loyalty, but more often it is because of frustrations with bureaucratic systems, frustrations at a particular person or bewilderment at how to communicate and relate. So much of the human conditions are made more difficult because of our inability to work together peacefully.

These aspects of church life can help people weather the storm of frustrated relationships. Discipleship training simply means helping people grow in the faith. They learn the Bible, understand theology and relationships within the church and they grow in grace. Christians have gained a great number of tools to do discipleship training well. The church that seeks to grow and reach more people for Christ has to learn to do discipleship training in an effective way. The second aspect is clear involvement, or helping every person understand that their task is to be a part of the life of the church. First Corinthians 12 describes us as the body, each one of us functioning in our own kind of way but as a part of the whole and dependent on one another. Finally a care program, for when emergencies happen and problems develop, is critical for a healthy church.

These concepts of discipleship, involvement and care are intermixed, interrelated and a part of the total life of a church. However, there are particular ways where each of the three is developed. Discipleship can be expressed in worship services, church Sunday school classes, Bible study groups, special training classes, lay theological education, prayer groups and spiritual retreats. The church needs to be very intentional about helping its members grow spiritually and in their knowledge of the faith. Too many times evangelism becomes an entry and there is no growth, spiritual development or maturity following the decision to accept and follow Christ. The church needs to intentionally provide a curriculum and have wholesome Bible study, clear theological education and answers to questions having to do with personal life issues such as family life, marriage, vocational decisions and knowledge of the spiritual disciplines such as prayer, Bible study and tithing.

There are basically seven steps that we want to encourage the new Christian to go through in the process of moving from someone who has not experienced the power of Christ in their life to someone who is actively involved in being an evangelist themselves.

Understand

The first step is to enable the new Christian to fully understand the experience of Christ. It has to do with discipleship, growth, training and encouraging. This step is a long process. You might even say we never complete it. It involves all the basics of becoming a fully-devoted follower of Christ, from biblical knowledge to knowledge of what it means to be the Church to the positive experiences of prayer and fellowship within the life of the church. However, as we are growing in the faith, we must begin to take the following other steps as well.

Following

Second, the individual clarifies and reinforces his decision to become a follower of Jesus Christ. It's that cognitive decision to say yes not only to the experience of accepting Christ as Savior but also accepting Christ as Lord. It is the process of saying, "We will take up our cross daily and follow." It is the behavioral, or doing, part of becoming a Christian disciple. It is easy to celebrate the joy of accepting Christ, the power of the experience of God's Holy Spirit, the joy of learning and growing and the peace that comes in true Christian fellowship. Yet, one of the deepest joys is the joy of following. Jesus concluded the Sermon on the Mount by saying, "Everyone who hears these words of mine and puts them into practice is like a wise man who built his house on the rock" (Matt. 7:24). To become an evangelist or someone who shares their faith, we must fully commit to the doing. If we don't, we become Christians only because of our acceptance and act of faith, not our behavior in our lives, and we miss out on many of the joys of the Christian faith.

Showing

The third step in this process is the decision is to be an evangelist; that is, to be willing to share our faith. When the disciples of Jesus asked their friends and family to follow Jesus, they were doing the natural thing. This is not to indicate that this number three step does not happen until one and two have happened. No, some of the best evangelists are brand new Christians! They have just found the joy of following Christ and they want to invite their friends, their family and their business associates. This decision to share the faith, to tell others about Jesus Christ, is an imperative that can be experienced as one of the very first parts of our becoming a follower of Christ. New Christians are fantastic in terms of their ability to understand their non-Christian or secular friends and know how to talk to them about Christ. Often, this is an uncomfortable thing for us to ask of new Christians. Some argue that it violates the new Christian's integrity of being a novice in the faith, but it is out of their very inexperience that they are able to share so clearly about Christ. The imperative is that we all share the faith, and the newest Christians are a part of that imperative.

Doing

The fourth step is the actual doing of the sharing and the activity that comes as a part of that. This can be exciting. It may be challenging. It is being a fully-devoted follower. The church and Christian friends in the church need to be actively supportive of the new Christian as they seek to be fishers of other people. The church needs to encourage, affirm, instruct and encourage.

Exploring

The fifth step is the process of learning how to explain the faith, what the church is all about, learning how the church does its work and how to articulate the simple act of committing to Christ. New Christians need to be committed to becoming lay theologians immediately. Classes can be lively opportunities for the new Christian to find a way of speaking about their faith more clearly and articulating the decision in a way that can be shared with their friends. Without instruction and good learning, the new Christian often becomes discouraged because they don't understand or they make mistakes that are hurtful. Consequently, they must learn as well as share.

Celebrating

Finally, the new Christian needs to be encouraged to celebrate. As we share with others, and they accept Christ, we need to understand the joy and the happiness of doing what Christ asked us to do, and following the Great Commission, and be joyful about sharing the faith. It is not some kind of hunting expedition that we celebrate; but it is a joyful sharing of what has changed our lives with friends and acquaintances.

Growing

The final step is that commitment the new Christian must make to continue growing, sharing and learning. It is a lifelong, joyful journey, and we need to be encouraged to be actively involved in all the ways that we can grow and be better, more effective and more articulate. Too many times in life, once we've accomplished a task, we leave it alone and move to a new challenge. Not so in moving the faith. We need to grow and learn and grow and learn over and over again.

Discipleship is commitment to Christ. We must teach and expect church members to be clearly and continually committed to Jesus Christ as Lord and Savior. Certainly, under the banner of evangelism, many of the above are not typically mentioned; but, without them, clear spiritual growth and discipleship, evangelistic efforts cannot bear any fruit. People end up going in the front door and out the back.

The second aspect, having to do with involvement, is a basic function of the church. Paul says in the twelfth chapter of Romans that we are all a part of the body; each one of us functions with Christ as the head. This involves two aspects of the churches life: one, we often call fellowship, and the other, service. Interestingly, these two aspects of involvement often happen together.

A group of men volunteered to be on the Habitat for Humanity team. They became best friends as they worked together to build houses for the poor, and their small community of 12 guys that work every Saturday building houses became a functioning part of the body of Christ. They cared for, helped, loved, supported, encouraged and affirmed each other—all those aspects of being a part of the church happened in that small Habitat for Humanity work team. Often, a fellowship group in the church such as a men's club takes on service capabilities. A certain men's group met once a month for a pancake breakfast, but they also met to do handyman tasks for elderly members of the church and other things like repair a dilapidated building at a local Salvation Army unit. Involvement in fellowship activities and service activities is an absolute necessity for people staying satisfied and growing in the life of a follower of Jesus Christ.

Care is crucial. One of the ironies of the church is that we focus on our call to help and care for people around the world; but, oftentimes, the people we neglect the most are those within the family of God, those church members who, because of the natural hurt of human life, struggle with making decisions and being successful. We need help. We need each other to listen and care. When we go to the hospital to have surgery, we need to know that our fellow church members are praying and listening and will be there with our spouse in the waiting room until the surgery is over. There are so many things that are absolute necessities in the life of the church, but one is to care for our own people. Regular calling, contacting, newsletters, email, Facebook—all are ways of networking together to be the church.

Questions for Discussion and Personal Reflection

1. How well does your church develop disciples?
2. How well does your church involve each individual?
3. How well does your church care for our people in times of difficulty?
4. Does your church help people at their point of need?
5. Discuss how to do the three above programs.
6. Spend time in prayer for ideas and motivation to do the above factors much better in your church.

Chapter 23
Conclusion—So Do It!

The biggest issue in evangelism in the church today is that we seem to be reluctant to do it. There are so many things to do. We can get involved in the community, have fellowship, devise and develop wonderful worship and have spiritual life retreats and keep ourselves busy in good ways. We can do all these and other "good things" but never really lead others to Christ.

The Last Thing He Asks Us to Do

The sad thing about this reality is that this evangelism is the last thing Jesus asked us to do. It is his final instruction. Most call it the Great Commission (Matt. 25:1b–20). Here, Jesus is with the disciples after the resurrection on the Mount of Olives. They are standing, talking and discussing. Jesus tells that He was going to leave. The picture is magnificent and has been made famous by artists through the centuries. It is a simple story of Jesus giving His final instruction. But why are we so reluctant to follow through?

They were in the midst of a difficult transition; Jesus had been killed, yet there He was resurrected. He had been with them, talked to them, advised them and encouraged them, but now He was giving them final instructions. His instructions were simple: Go and make disciples of everyone, teaching them what he had taught. Theologians call this the Great Commission. We need to understand that the situation for the disciples was not clear for them. They were confused and unsure of what to do afterwards. They met for days trying to decide how to interpret these last instructions. It was only when they gathered in Jerusalem in the Upper Room on the day of Pentecost that they finally understood what Christ had meant and put His instructions into practice. As Jesus' followers put his instructions into action on the streets of Jerusalem, a movement began that changed the world. "Go make disciples" is His instruction. The world still needs us to lead people to Jesus Christ.

Earlier in this book, I told the story of my mother's death and her last will and testament. My family and I were placed in a difficult situation at a difficult time. In a very real sense, we as Christians are always in that dilemma. Should we do what He told us to do? My brother, sister and I debated whether or not we should do what my mom had said to do. It was a simple note left in the dresser by her bed, but the repercussions of following through on it were complex. It meant work and effort and part of it seemed impractical, but we knew it was the right thing to do, so we did it. Maybe that is the way the Church needs to approach evangelism. Sometimes we don't want to do it; we would rather take care of things that are less frustrating and more comfortable to do. We think we have a better idea, a better task and a better understanding of what the Church ought to do. The church has debated over and over through the centuries: Should the emphasis be on growth or should it be upon ministry? Should the emphasis be on social justice and social issues or individual salvation? We have spent years, if not decades, debating and fighting. We have created new denominations and new groups. We have started new individual churches trying to proclaim the right emphasis. But this is what Jesus said to do–"Go Make Disciples." There is no question about it; there is no debate about it. He told us to do it. These were the last words He said. As he began his ministry, He said to several fishermen, *"Come with me and I will make you fishers of men"* (Matt. 4:19). Maybe it is that simple; we are told to go fish. We are told to make disciples.

A New Promise

Churches have a variety of things that they ask people to promise when they become Christians. After that commitment to Christ has been made clear, most churches ask people to assume responsibilities in the church. In the United Methodist Church, in the past you have been asked, "Will you support the church with your prayers, presence, gifts and service?" These vows instruct a disciple of Christ to pray, attend, give and serve. This is a good summary of what it is to be a Christian, yet in the most recent judicatory meeting of the United Methodist church a fifth requirement was added. The addition asks that the Christian support the church by witnessing. The new promise asks us to be evangelistic in the midst of the enthusiasm that we all feel for Christ. The requirement is to share the faith. Will the Christian do as Jesus said in His last instructions, make disciples and teach what He taught to the world? To intentionally include "witness" as part of membership vows creates a new priority for any church.

In a time when the culture is very secular and the Church's influence has declined; in a time when so many people have not heard the Gospel and do not know about Jesus; in a time when the world needs the kind of loving justice and truth that Jesus taught, the Christian must take responsibility to share and lead. This must be a priority.

The idea of TELL is simply that we must tell people about Jesus Christ. Telling is a simple concept, but its execution is far from simple. Telling involves the truth of our own lives and our church; it involves explaining what Jesus taught and what we believe. Telling is living what we explain and being examples of Christ's love in the world. Finally, telling is enthusiastically leading people to the church and to commit to Christ.

As you come to the end of this view of witnessing and sharing the faith, my question is clear. Will you do what Jesus asked? Will you tell? Will you tell how the power of God has changed your life? Will you explain the teachings of Jesus in a way that your friends can understand? Will you live your faith? When you make a mistake and do something that you know you shouldn't have done, will you do everything you realistically can to make the corrections and not do it again? Will you be an example of a follower of Jesus? Will you lead people to know Christ, know the church and make a commitment to Christ? Will you not only understand but give your life? Will you be an evangelist?

A New Priority

There are all kinds of methodologies, plans and strategies. This book aims to offer some ideas that can be helpful, but many others have dealt with the same topic with their own enthusiasm. Great leaders in the Church have developed and written on many great ideas and understandings of witnessing and sharing the faith. Certainly, the ideas expressed in this book entitled *TELL* offer some clear understandings of how to witness in the contemporary, secular world in which we live, but the real question is not, "How do you share your faith?" but "Will you share the faith? Will you do your best?" The final instruction: Go, make disciples. Our final response: I will do it!

Questions for Discussion and Personal Reflection

1. Are you telling the story of what God has done for you to others? How? When?
2. Are you telling about Christ by answering the hard questions of faith, theology and the Bible? Are you a teacher and explainer of the faith?
3. Are you living an authentic life following Christ? Do your friends and family see Christ in you?
4. Are you a leader, leading people to know God's love, follow in the steps of Jesus and become part of His church?
5. Spend time asking God to help you and your church become more evangelistic.

Appendix
Bibliography and Suggested Reading

Abraham, William J. The Logic of Evangelism. Grand Rapids, MI : Eerdmans, 1989.

Adeney, Frances. Graceful Evangelism. Grand Rapids, MI: Baker Academic, 2010.

Anderson, Douglas and Michael Coyner. The Race to Reach Out. Nashville, TN: Abingdon, 2004.

Barna, George. Grow Your Church From the Outside In. Ventura, CA: Regal Books, 2002.

Barna, George. Revolution. Carol Stream, IL: Tyndale, 2005.

Barrs, Jerram. Learning Evangelism from Jesus. Wheaton, IL Crossway, 2009.

Barrs, Jerram. The Heart of Evangelism. Wheaton, IL Crossway, 2001.

Bechtle, Mike. Evangelism for the Rest of Us. Grand Rapids, MI: Baker Books, 2006.

Brunner, Emil. The Divine Imperative. Westminster John Knox Pr, 1979.

Chesnut, Robert. Transforming the Mainline Church. Buena Park, California: Geneva, 2000.

Compton, Stephen. Rekindling the Mainline. Herndon, VA: The Alban Institute, 2003.

Fensham, Charles. Emerging from the Dark Age Ahead. Toronto, Ontario, Canada: Novalis, 2008.

Fox, Eddie, and George Morris. Faith-Sharing. Nashville, TN: Discipleship Resources, 1996.

Frankl, Viktor. Man's Search for Meaning. Boston, MA : Beacon, 2000.

Gary Sweeten, Dave Ping, and Anne Clippard. Listening for Heavens' Sake. Cincinnati, OH: Teleios Publications, 1993

Getz, Gene and Joe Wall. Effective Church Growth Strategies. Nashville, TN: Word, 2000.

Gonnerman, Frederick. Getting the Word Out. Herndon, VA: The Alban Institute, 1989.

Grenz, Stanley J. A Primer on Postmodernism. Grand Rapids, MI: Eerdmans Publishing Co., 1996.

Groeschel, Craig. It. Grand Rapids, MI: Zondervan, 2008.

Hamilton, Adam. Leading Beyond the Walls. Nashville, TN: Abingdon, 2002.

Henderson, Jim, and Matt Casper. Jim and Casper Go to Church. Carol Stream, IL: Barna Books, 2007.

Hunter, George G. III. How to Reach Secular People. Nashville, TN: Abingdon, 1992.

Hunter, George G. III. Radical Outreach. Nashville, TN: Abingdon, 2003.

Hunter, George G. III. The Celtic Way of Evangelism. Nashville, TN: Abingdon, 2000.

Hybels, Bill and Mark Mittelberg. Becoming a Contagious Christian. Grand Rapids, MI: Zondervan, 1995.

Hybels, Bill. Just Walk Across the Room: Simple Steps Pointing People to Faith. Grand Rapids, MI: Zondervan, 2006.

Jones, Scott. The Evangelistic Love of God and Neighbor. Nashville, TN: Abingdon, 2003.

Kimball, Dan. I Like Jesus but Not the Church. Grand Rapids, MI: Zondervan, 2005.

Kimball, Dan. They Like Jesus but not the Church. Grand Rapids, MI: Zondervan, 2007.

Kinnaman, David and Gabe Lyons. Unchristian. Grand Rapids, MI: Baker Books, 2009.

Krattenmaker, Tom. "How to sell Christianity? Ask an atheist." USA Today 27 June 2010.

McLaren, Brian D. A New Kind of Christian: A Tale of Two Friends on a Spiritual Journey. Hoboken, NJ: Jossey -Bass, 2001.

McLaren, Brian. A New Kind of Christian. Hoboken, NJ: Jossey-Bass, 2001.

McLaren, Brian. More Ready Than You Realize. Grand Rapids, MI: Zondervan, 2002.

McNeal, Reggie. The Present Future. Hoboken, NJ: Jossey -Bass, 2003.

Miller, Donald. Searching for God Knows What. Nashville, TN: Nelson, 2004.

Mittelberg, Mark. Bulding a Contagious Church. Grand Rapids, MI: Zondervan, 2000.

Newman, Randy. Questioning Evangelism. Grand Rapids, MI : Kregal, 2004.

Oden, Thomas. Turning Around the Mainline. Grand Rapids, MI: Baker Books, 2006.

Pagitt, Doug and Tom Jones. An Emergent Manifesto of Hope. Grand Rapids, MI: Baker Books, 2007.

Peterson, Jim. Living Proof. Colorado Springs, CO : Navpress, 1989.

Pierson, Robert. Needs-Based Evangelism. Nashville, TN: Abingdon, 2006.

Putnam, Robert D. Bowling Alone: The Collapse and Revival of American Community. New York, NY: Simon and Schuster, 2000.

Rainer, Thom and Eric Geiger. Simple Church. Nashville, TN: B&H Publishing Group, 2006.

Rainer, Thom. Surprising Insights from the Unchurched and Proven Ways to Reach Them. Grand Rapids, MI: Zondervan, 2001.

Ramsey, Norman. Moving at the Speed of Grace. Mustang, OK: Tate, 2010.

Reid, Alvin. Radically Unchurched. Grand Rapids, MI : Kregal, 2002.

Reising, Richard. Church Marketing 101. Grand Rapids, MI: Baker Books, 2006.

Richardson, Rick. Evangelism Outside the Box. Downers Grove, IL: InterVarsity Press, 2000.

Roberts, Bob, Jr. The Multiplying Church. Grand Rapids, MI: Zondervan, 2008.

Roxburgh, Alan and M. Scott Boren. Introducing the Missional Church. Grand Rapids, MI: Baker Books, 2009.

Sheldon, Charles. In His Steps. Uhrichsville, OH: Barbout, 2002.

Sjogren, Steve, Dave Ping, and Doug Pollock. Irresistible Evangelism. Loveland, CO: Group, 2004.

Southwick, John. (June 2010). Beyond the Usual Slice of the Pie II. Background Data for Mission, 22(6).

Spiedel, Royal. Evangelism in the Small Membership Church. Nashville, TN: Abingdon, 2007.

Sweet, Leonard. Carpe Mañana. Grand Rapids, MI: Zondervan, 2001.

Tuttle, Robert. Can We Talk? Nashville, TN: Nashville, TN: Abingdon, 1999.

Waltz, Mark. First Impressions. Loveland, CO: Group Publishing, 2005.

Wright, Linda Raney. Christianity's Crisis in Evangelism. Gresham, OR: Vision House, 1995.

What Others Say About "Tell"

Tell addresses the crucial problem that keeps the church from being missionally effective: more Christians need to tell the good news of Christ. Bob Pierson's account of why we tell, how we tell, and what to tell is shared with personal illustrations and great clarity. He outlines the complexities of the evangelistic task and offers concrete ideas of how to address them. This book is theologically sound, practically oriented, and engagingly written!

Bishop Scott Jones,
Resident Bishop of the Kansas Area of the United Methodist Church

Bob Pierson understands the theory of ministry in that he knows why faithful pastors do what they do. But more than that, Pierson communicates the art, science, or practice of personal evangelism as lived out in churches. He does what seminaries would do if they had more time or know-how. About this book all I can counsel is to do as Augustine suggested: "Take up and read, take up and read" (Tolle lege, tolle lege). —Confessions, Book VIII, Chapter 12

David N. Mosser,
Author of Westminister John Knox book *Transitions* and editor of *The Abingdon Preaching Annual.*

In a time when the Church needs to sound a clarion call to offer Christ to a hurting and broken world, Bob Pierson offers a clear voice. With clarity, practicality, and joy, Bob leads us toward a clear and certain future in Jesus Christ. At last, a tool to equip God's people in evangelism and mission! Now is the time. Tell *is the resource. Thank you, Bob, for such a practical gift to the Church!*

Bill McAlilly,
Seashore District Superintendent
Mississippi Conference of the United Methodist Church

What Others Say About "Tell"

You will find, as you read the book, Tell, *by Bob Pierson, words that convey the joy of sharing a faith that transforms lives. He says, "I cannot imagine anything more joyful, more powerful, and more peaceful than serving God with my heart, mind, soul and body." And he emphasizes that people do not come to the faith from guilt or fear but from seeing in another the hope and love of God.*

Bob writes as he talks and his stories enliven the text. In each chapter, key points are broken down into smaller components that help the reader understand better the intention of the whole. The book falls into two parts that mirror one another through story and instruction: the first part is a guide for individuals in telling their faith. The second is a guide for congregations in telling the faith. Both are necessary since the command to witness is individual and corporate through the church – the body of Christ.

Tell *is not just about words. Bob Pierson recognizes the power of actions that match our words of faith. Use the questions and suggestions found at the end of each chapter to equip yourself and others for witness to others of a faith that brings joy to life.*

Rev. MaryJane Pierce Norton,
Associate General Secretary
Leadership Ministries
GBOD | The United Methodist Church

Bob Pierson, once again, offers a gift to the church. In Tell, *he invites and instructs how to share the story that changes lives, households and communities. Read it to change and be changed.*

Vance Ross,
Associate General Secretary